School, Family, and Community Partnerships

School, Family, and Community Partnerships

Your Handbook for Action

Joyce L. Epstein, Lucretia Coates,
Karen Clark Salinas,
Mavis G. Sanders, Beth S. Simon

CORWIN PRESS, INC.
A Sage Publications Company
Thousand Oaks, California

For information:

 Corwin Press, Inc.
A Sage Publications Company
2455 Teller Road
Thousand Oaks, California 91320
E-mail: order@corwin.sagepub.com

SAGE Publications Ltd.
6 Bonhill Street
London EC2A 4PU
United Kingdom

SAGE Publications India Pvt. Ltd.
M-32 Market
Greater Kailash I
New Delhi 110 048 India

Printed in the United States of America

Library of Congress Cataloging-in-Publication Data

School, family, and community partnerships: Your handbook for action
/ Joyce L. Epstein ... [et al.].
   p. cm.
  Includes bibliographical references.
  ISBN 0-8039-6570-2 (cloth: acid-free paper). — ISBN
0-8039-6571-0 (pbk.: acid-free paper)
  1. Community and school—United States. 2. Home and school—
United States. 3. School improvement programs—United States.
I. Epstein, Joyce Levy.
LC221.S366 1997
371.19—dc21   97-21052

This book is printed on acid-free paper.

   98 99 00 01 02 10 9 8 7 6 5 4 3 2

Production Editor: Sanford Robinson
Editorial Assistant: Kristen L. Gibson
Production Assistant: Karen Wiley
Typesetter: Rebecca Evans
Cover Designer: Marcia M. Rosenburg

Contents

Acknowledgments   vii

About the Authors   ix

Introduction   xi

1. A Comprehensive Framework for School, Family, and Community Partnerships   1

Caring for the Children We Share   2

Overlapping Spheres of Influence: Understanding the Theory   3

How Partnerships Work in Practice   5

What Research Says   6

Six Types of Involvement—Six Types of Caring   7

Action Teams for School, Family, and Community Partnerships   12

Characteristics of Successful Programs   17

Next Steps: Strengthening Partnerships   21

2. Using the Framework in Practice: Stories From the Field   26

Baltimore's Story: Finding the Keys to School, Family, and Community Partnerships   28

School Stories: Examples of the Six Types of Involvement   34

Type 1: Parenting   34

Type 2: Communicating   36

Type 3: Volunteering   38

Type 4: Learning at Home   40

Type 5: Decision Making   42

Type 6: Collaborating With the Community   44

3. Conducting Workshops   46

Training Workshops   47

Sample Agendas for Training Workshops   49

Components of Training Workshops   52

Sample Agenda for End-of-Year Celebration Workshop   60

End-of-Year Celebration Workshop: Notes for Facilitators   64

Sample Workshop Evaluations   67

4. Materials for Presentations and Workshops   **69**

    Theoretical Model of Overlapping Spheres of Influence   72
    Keys to Successful Partnerships   74
      Sample Practices   82
      Challenges and Redefinitions   88
    Summaries of the Six Types of School, Family,
      and Community Partnerships   94
    Ten Steps to School-Family-Community Partnerships   100
    Action Team Structure   101
    Members of the Action Team   103
    The ABCs of Action Team Leadership   104
    Understanding Levels of Commitment   112
    What Questions Must Be Asked?   113
    District Leadership Roles   117
    State Leadership Roles   118

5. Planning and Evaluation Forms   **119**

    Starting Points: An Inventory of Present Practices   122
    Three-Year Outlines—Forms A and B   126
    One-Year Action Plans—Forms A and B   130
    End-of-Year Evaluation   137

**6. Other Helpful Forms for Developing
Programs of Partnership**   **144**

    What Do Facilitators Do?   146
    Checklist: Are You Ready?   147
    Who Are the Members of the Action Team?   148
    Small Group Discussion Guide   151
    School Goals and Results of Partnerships   156
    Linking Practices With Results   158
    Summary of School Visits   161
    Gathering Good Ideas   163
    Transitions: Involving Families When Students Move to
      New Schools   167
    Sample Pledges or Contracts   170

**7. More Information on Middle and High Schools,
Homework, and Surveys**   **175**

    Reports on Partnerships in the Middle Grades and
      High Schools   176
    Teachers Involve Parents in Schoolwork (TIPS) Processes   199
    Surveys and Summaries: Questionnaires on School and
      Family Partnerships   210

8. Networking for Best Results   **213**

    National Network of Partnership-2000 Schools   215
    Sharing Best Practices   217
    Workshops for Key Contacts   226

    Suggested Readings   227
    Ordering Information   231

Acknowledgments

T he authors acknowledge the assistance and contributions of Jerry Baum, Executive Director of the Fund for Educational Excellence, Lori Connors-Tadros, Susan C. Herrick, and John H. Hollifield at the educational research center at Johns Hopkins University. We also appreciate the efforts of countless teachers, administrators, parents, and students who have worked with us over the years to help design, implement, test, and improve the ideas that are included in this handbook.

Special acknowledgments are due the Baltimore City Public School (BCPS) teachers who contributed information for the reports on activities in Chapter 2: Charlene Bratton, Jackie Griswold, Adele Israel, and Gita Lefstein; Marsha Powell-Johnson, Brenda Thomas, and Paula Williams, who facilitate the efforts of over 75 BCPS schools to develop their programs of partnership; and BCPS Area Superintendents Gary Thrift, Clifton Ball, and Sandra Wighton, who have helped their schools and the researchers understand how district-level leadership works hand in hand with school and community leaders for school improvement.

Thanks also go to state leaders Gary Lloyd in Utah, Jane Grinde and Ruth Anne Landsverk in Wisconsin, and Irene Hechler and Mary Wilmer in Maryland for demonstrating how state leadership can be structured in various ways to help districts help schools help families help students. Many thanks, too, to the other "lead" states, districts, and schools who have joined the Center's National Network of Partnership-2000 Schools to use and adapt this handbook to build better programs of school, family, and community partnerships. Finally, we acknowledge Nick Foudos, who designed the logo for the National Network which appears on the cover of this handbook.

This work is supported by grants from the Office of Educational Research and Improvement (OERI) of the U.S. Department of Education to the researchers at Johns Hopkins University's Center for Research on the Education of Students Placed at Risk (CRESPAR), from the Lilly Endowment to the Center on School, Family, and Community

Partnerships, and previous grants from the Edna McConnell Clark Foundation and Leon Lowenstein Foundation. It also is supported by grants to the Fund for Educational Excellence from the Aaron Straus and Lillie Straus Foundation, Goldsmith Family Foundation, and Morris Goldseker Foundation of Maryland. The perspectives are the authors' and do not necessarily represent the policies or positions of the funding agencies.

We gratefully acknowledge the following for permission to reprint:

Chapter 1:

Epstein, Joyce L. (1995). School/family/community partnerships: Caring for the children we share. *Phi Delta Kappan, 76,* 701-712.

Chapter 7:

Connors, Lori J., & Epstein, Joyce L. (1994). *Taking stock: Views of teachers, parents, and students on school, family, and community partnerships in high schools.* Report 25. Baltimore: Center on Families, Communities, Schools and Children's Learning at Johns Hopkins University.

Epstein, Joyce L. (1992). Teachers Involve Parents in Schoolwork (TIPS): Involving families to improve student achievement. In C. Hyman (Ed.), *The school-community cookbook* (pp. 176-182). Baltimore: Fund for Educational Excellence.

Epstein, Joyce L., & Connors, Lori J. (June, 1992). School and family partnerships (for middle grades and high schools). *NASSP Practitioner, 18*(4).

Research and Development Report, No. 4. (September, 1993). Surveys and summaries help schools identify and analyze current practices of partnership; develop more comprehensive programs (John H. Hollifield, ed.). Baltimore: Center on Families, Communities, Schools and Children's Learning, Johns Hopkins University.

Research and Development Report, No. 5. (June, 1994). High schools gear up to create effective school and family partnerships (John H. Hollifield, ed.). Baltimore: Center on Families, Communities, Schools and Children's Learning, Johns Hopkins University.

About the Authors

Joyce L. Epstein, Ph.D. in sociology from Johns Hopkins University, is Director of the Center on School, Family, and Community Partnerships and the National Network of Partnership-2000 Schools, Principal Research Scientist in the Center for Research on the Education of Students Placed at Risk (CRESPAR), and Professor of Sociology at Johns Hopkins University. She has over one hundred publications on the organization and effects of school, classroom, family, and peer environments, with many focused on school, family, and community connections. In 1995, she established the National Network of Partnership-2000 Schools to demonstrate the important intersections of research, policy, and practice for school improvement. She serves on numerous editorial boards and advisory panels on parent involvement, middle grades education, and school reform. She is recipient of the Academy for Educational Development's 1991 Alvin C. Eurich Education Award for her work on family-school partnerships.

Lucretia Coates, M.A. in education from Morgan State University, is Principal at the Dr. Bernard Harris, Sr. Elementary School in Baltimore, Maryland. For eight years she worked with researchers and educators to develop and implement the Baltimore School and Family Connections project that led to the National Network of Partnership-2000 Schools. In addition to writing sections of this handbook, she has formulated and edited a newsletter to help Baltimore City Public Schools to share progress on partnerships, trained and assisted about 50 Action Teams for School, Family, and Community Partnerships in Baltimore, trained facilitators to help other schools, and presented information on partnerships at numerous conferences in cities and states in the United States. She also is coauthor of an article on the effects on students and parents of summer home learning packets.

Karen Clark Salinas, M.S.W. in social work from the University of North Carolina, Chapel Hill, is Senior Research Assistant at the Center on School, Family, and Community Partnerships and the Center for Research on the Education of Students Placed at Risk (CRESPAR) at Johns Hopkins University. She is coauthor of the inventory "Starting Points" that helps schools identify their present practices of partnership, the Teachers Involve Parents in Schoolwork (TIPS) manuals and prototype interactive homework materials, surveys of teacher, parent, and student views on partnerships, and a book *Promising Practices in the Middle Grades.* She is Communications Director of the National Network of Partnership-2000 Schools, edits the newsletter *Type 2,* and coordinates training workshops for members of the Network.

Mavis G. Sanders, Ph.D. in education from Stanford University, is Associate Research Scientist at the Center for Research on the Education of Students Placed at Risk (CRESPAR), and Assistant Director of the Center on School, Family, and Community Partnerships and the National Network of Partnership-2000 Schools at Johns Hopkins University. She has authored articles on the effects of school, family, and community support on African American adolescents' school success, and case studies of schools in Baltimore that are working to develop their partnership programs. She also coauthored a review of international studies of school, family, and community connections and other publications on partnerships. She is interested in how schools involve families that are traditionally hard to reach, how Action Teams meet challenges for implementing excellent programs and practices, and how schools define "community" and develop meaningful school-family-community connections.

Beth S. Simon, M.A. in sociology from Johns Hopkins University (JHU), is a doctoral candidate in the Department of Sociology at JHU. She is Dissemination Director of the National Network of Partnership-2000 Schools, overseeing the distribution and collection of membership forms and data for the Network, and is designer and manager of the Network's web site. She is conducting research on the effects of interactive homework on student learning in the middle grades and on patterns of participation of states, districts, and schools in the National Network of Partnership-2000 Schools. Her other interests include school, classroom, and family effects on student success.

Introduction

There is no topic in education on which there is greater agreement than the need for "parent involvement." Everyone wants it, but most do not know *how* to develop productive *programs* of school-family-community partnerships.

To enable families and communities to become informed about and involved in children's education and in the schools, partnerships must be viewed as an essential component of school organization that influences student development and learning, rather than as an optional activity or a matter of public relations. It takes time, organization, and effort to develop a good program.

Over the past decade, researchers, educators, parents, students, community members, and others have worked together to learn how to help all elementary, middle, and high schools to develop and maintain programs of partnership. Now, all schools can design and conduct school, home, and community connections in ways that improve schools, strengthen families, and increase student success. It is time for action.

This handbook will enable state, district, and school leaders to organize and implement positive and permanent programs of school, family, and community partnerships. The handbook focuses on schools because that is where the children are. It is designed to guide the work of Action Teams for School, Family, and Community Partnerships consisting of principals, teachers, parents, and others. The information, forms, and activities also will help state and district leaders support, facilitate, and reward the work of their schools. The handbook's eight chapters offer step-by-step strategies to improve school-family-community connections:

- **Chapter 1: Background and Framework.** Summarizes the theory and research on which the handbook is based, describes the framework of six types of involvement, and discusses the Action Team approach for developing a comprehensive program of partnerships. Charts in this chapter identify sample practices, challenges that must be met for a successful program, and results that can be expected for each type of involvement.

- **Chapter 2: Practical Applications.** Illustrates how the components of the program are applied at the district and school levels. Stories from the field feature the work of a district level facilitator and reports of sample activities for each of the six types of involvement.

- **Chapter 3: Workshops.** Outlines agendas for short and extended training workshops and end-of-year celebrations that district and state leaders may conduct to help Action Teams for School, Family, and Community Partnerships write plans, share best practices, solve problems, and continue program development.

- **Chapter 4: Reproducibles.** Supplies the charts and diagrams that can be used as transparencies or handouts in presentations and workshops to share the background, framework, and structure of the program.

- **Chapter 5: Plans and Progress.** Includes an inventory of present practices, three-year outlines, one-year action plans, and evaluation forms to establish and continue the program. These forms are updated each year to continually improve partnerships and link practices to school improvement goals.

- **Chapter 6: Group Activities.** Contains discussion topics, worksheets, and other forms that support and advance the work of Action Teams, district facilitators, and state coordinators.

- **Chapter 7: Special Topics.** Presents additional information for middle and high schools, introduces interactive homework, and summarizes survey instruments.

- **Chapter 8: Networking.** Indicates how readers of the handbook can join other schools, districts, and states in the National Network of Partnership-2000 Schools at Johns Hopkins University to obtain information and assistance, and share ideas and progress.

The handbook is based on knowledge that we have gained over many years talking and working with hundreds of teachers and administrators and thousands of families and students in many schools, towns, and cities. In schools at all levels, teachers and administrators want to know how to work with families in positive ways. Parents want to know how to help their children succeed in school, how to recognize and ensure high-quality education for their children, and how to support and improve school programs. Students want to succeed in school but often need guidance and encouragement from many sources. These different needs and interests can be met in programs of school-family-community partnerships that encourage all who are interested in children to work effectively together.

The handbook provides a basic structure and useful guidelines that schools can use to organize a comprehensive program of partnerships. Educators, families, students, and community members will work together to select and tailor activities to meet their needs, interests, and goals. Over time, new practices, creative ideas, and unique approaches will be integrated in each school's program.

Excellent partnership programs inform and involve all families, at all grade levels, include students and the community, are family-friendly, have clear goals, document results for students, families, and schools, and continue from year to year. The structures and processes presented in this handbook have been tested, materials have been developed and improved, and information has expanded from the elementary to the high school years. We encourage readers to use these tools to build comprehensive, inclusive, and permanent programs of school-family-community partnerships.

1

A Comprehensive Framework for School, Family, and Community Partnerships

This chapter summarizes a theory of *overlapping spheres of influence* to explain the shared responsibilities of home, school, and community for children's learning and development. It also charts the six types of involvement, the challenges they pose, new definitions, and the expected results of well-designed and well-implemented practices.

The chapter describes realistic strategies that you can use to develop and maintain comprehensive programs of partnership to support and increase student success. It describes the work that all Action Teams for School, Family, and Community Partnerships will do to plan, implement, and oversee activities for productive home-school-community connections. Each Action Team also monitors its progress and works to improve practices to meet the needs and interests of its students, families, and school.

This chapter provides background information that will help you understand the "big picture" of positive school-family-community partnerships.

An earlier version of this chapter appeared as an article in *Phi Delta Kappan,* 77(9), May 1995, pp. 701-712.

Caring for the Children We Share

Joyce L. Epstein

The way schools care about children is reflected in the way schools care about the children's families. If educators view children simply as *students,* they are likely to see the family as separate from the school. That is, the family is expected to do its job and leave the education of children to the schools. If educators view students as *children,* they are likely to see both the family and the community as partners with the school in children's education and development. Partners recognize their shared interests in and responsibilities for children, and they work together to create better programs and opportunities for students.

There are many reasons for developing school, family, and community partnerships. They can improve school programs and school climate, provide family services and support, increase parents' skills and leadership, connect families with others in the school and in the community, and help teachers with their work. However, the main reason to create such partnerships is to help all youngsters succeed in school and in later life. When parents, teachers, students, and others view one another as partners in education, a caring community forms around students and begins its work.

What do successful partnership programs look like? How can practices be effectively designed and implemented? What are the results of better communications, interactions, and exchanges across these three important contexts? These questions have challenged research and practice, creating an interdisciplinary field of inquiry into school, family, and community partnerships with "caring" as a core concept.

The field has been strengthened by supporting federal, state, and local policies. For example, the Goals 2000 legislation sets partnerships as a voluntary national goal for all schools; Title I specifies and mandates programs and practices of partnership in order for schools to qualify for or maintain funding. Many states and districts have developed or are preparing policies to guide schools in creating more systematic connections with families and communities. These policies reflect research results and the prior successes of leading educators who have shown that these goals are attainable.

Underlying these policies and programs is a theory of how social organizations connect; a framework of the basic components of school, family, and community partnerships for children's learning; a growing literature on the positive and negative results of these connections for students, families, and schools; and an understanding of how to organize good programs. In this chapter, I summarize the theory, framework, and guidelines that have assisted the schools in our research projects in building partnerships and that should help any elementary, middle, or high school take similar steps.

Overlapping Spheres of Influence: Understanding the Theory

Schools make choices. They might conduct only a few communications and interactions with families and communities, keeping the three spheres of influence that directly affect student learning and development relatively separate. Or they might conduct many high-quality communications and interactions designed to bring all three spheres of influence closer together. With frequent interactions between schools, families, and communities, more students are more likely to receive common messages from various people about the importance of school, of working hard, of thinking creatively, of helping one another, and of staying in school.

The *external* model of overlapping spheres of influence recognizes that the three major contexts in which students learn and grow—the family, the school, and the community—may be drawn together or pushed apart. In this model, there are some practices that schools, families, and communities conduct separately and some that they conduct jointly in order to influence children's learning and development. The *internal* model of the interaction of the three spheres of influence shows where and how complex and essential interpersonal relations and patterns of influence occur between individuals at home, at school, and in the community. These social relationships may be enacted and studied at an *institutional* level (e.g., when a school invites all families to an event or sends the same communications to all families) and at an *individual* level (e.g., when a parent and a teacher meet in conference or talk by phone). Connections between schools or parents and community groups, agencies, and services can also be represented and studied within the model.[1]

The model of school, family, and community partnerships locates the student at the center. The inarguable fact is that students are the main actors in their education, development, and success in school. School, family, and community partnerships cannot simply produce successful students. Rather, partnership activities may be designed to engage, guide, energize, and motivate students to produce their own successes. The assumption is that if children feel cared for and encouraged to work hard in the role of student they are more likely to do their best to learn to read, write, calculate, and learn other skills and talents and to remain in school.

Interestingly and somewhat ironically, studies indicate that students are also crucial for the success of school, family, and community partnerships. Students are often their parents' main source of information about school. In strong partnership programs, teachers help students understand and conduct traditional communications with families (e.g., delivering memos or report cards) and new communications (e.g., interacting with family members about homework or participating in parent-teacher-student conferences). As we gain more information about the role of students in partnerships, we are developing a more complete understanding of how schools, families, and communities must work with students to increase their chances for success.

How Theory Sounds in Practice

In some schools, there are still educators who say, "If the family would just do its job, we could do our job." And there are still families who say, "I raised this child; now it is your job to educate her." These words embody the theory of "separate spheres of influence." Other educators say, "I cannot do my job without the help of my students' families and the support of this community." And some parents say, "I really need to know what is happening in school in order to help my child." These phrases embody the theory of "overlapping spheres of influence."

In a partnership, teachers and administrators create more *family-like* schools. A family-like school recognizes each child's individuality and makes each child feel special and included. Family-like schools welcome all families, not just those that are easy to reach. In a partnership, parents create more *school-like* families. A school-like family recognizes that each child is also a student. Families reinforce the importance of school, homework, and activities that build student skills and feelings of success. Communities, including groups of parents working together, create school-like opportunities, events, and programs that reinforce, recognize, and reward students for good progress, creativity, contributions, and excellence. Communities also create *family-like* settings, services, and events to enable families to better support their children. *Community-minded* families and students help their neighborhoods and other families. The concept of a community school is re-emerging. It refers to a place where programs and services for students, parents, and others are offered before, during, and after the regular school day.

Schools and communities talk about programs and services that are "family-friendly"—meaning that they take into account the needs and realities of family life in the 1990s, are feasible to conduct, and are equitable toward all families. When all these concepts combine, children experience *learning communities* or *caring communities*.[2]

All these terms are consistent with the theory of overlapping spheres of influence, but they are not abstract concepts. You will find them daily in conversations, news stories, and celebrations of many kinds. In a family-like school, a teacher might say, "I know when a student is having a bad day and how to help him along." A student might slip and call a teacher "mom" or "dad" and then laugh with a mixture of embarrassment and glee. In a school-like family, a parent might say, "I make sure my daughter knows that homework comes first." A boy might raise his hand to speak at the dinner table and then joke about acting as if he were still in school. When communities reach out to students and their families, youngsters might say, "This program really made my schoolwork make sense!" Parents or educators might comment, "This community really supports its schools."

Once people hear about such concepts as family-like schools or school-like families, they remember positive examples of schools, teachers, and places in the community that were "like a family" to them. They may remember how a teacher paid individual attention to them, recognized their uniqueness, or praised them for real progress, just as a parent might. Or they might recall things at home that were "just like school" and supported their work as a student, or they might remember community activities that made them feel smart or good about themselves and their families. They will recall that parents, siblings, and other family members engaged in and enjoyed educational activities and took pride in the good schoolwork or homework that they did, just as a teacher might.

How Partnerships Work in Practice

These terms and examples are evidence of the *potential* for schools, families, and communities to create caring educational environments. It is possible to have a school that is excellent academically but ignores families. However, that school will build barriers between teachers, parents, and children—barriers that affect school life and learning. It is possible to have a school that is ineffective academically but involves families in many good ways. With its weak academic program, that school will shortchange students' learning. Neither of these schools exemplifies a caring, educational environment that requires academic excellence, good communication, and productive interactions involving school, family, and community.

Some children succeed in school without much family involvement or despite family neglect or distress, particularly if the school has excellent academic and support programs. Teachers, relatives outside the immediate family, other families, and members of the community can provide important guidance and encouragement to these students. As support from school, family, and community accumulates, significantly more students feel secure and cared for, understand the goals of education, work to achieve to their full potential, build positive attitudes and school behaviors, and stay in school. The shared interests and investments of schools, families, and communities create the conditions of caring that work to "overdetermine" the likelihood of student success.[3]

Any practice can be designed and implemented well or poorly. And even well-implemented partnership practices may not be useful to all families. In a caring school community, participants work continually to improve the nature and effects of partnerships. Although the interactions of educators, parents, students, and community members will not always be smooth or successful, partnership programs establish a base of respect and trust on which to build. Good partnerships with-stand questions, conflicts, debates, and disagreements; provide structures and processes to solve problems; and are maintained—even strengthened—after differences have been resolved. Without this firm base, disagreements and problems that are sure to arise about schools and students will be harder to solve.

What Research Says

In surveys and field studies involving teachers, parents, and students at the elementary, middle, and high school levels, some important patterns relating to partnerships have emerged.[4]

- Partnerships tend to decline across the grades, *unless* schools and teachers work to develop and implement appropriate practices of partnership at each grade level.

- Affluent communities currently have more positive family involvement, on average, *unless* schools and teachers in economically distressed communities work to build positive partnerships with their students' families.

- Schools in more economically depressed communities make more contacts with families about the problems and difficulties their children are having, *unless* they work at developing balanced partnership programs that include contacts about positive accomplishments of students.

- Single parents, parents who are employed outside the home, parents who live far from the school, and fathers are less involved, on average, at the school building, *unless* the school organizes opportunities for families to volunteer at various times and in various places to support the school and their children.

Researchers have also drawn the following conclusions:

- Just about all families care about their children, want them to succeed, and are eager to obtain better information from schools and communities so as to remain good partners in their children's education.

- Just about all teachers and administrators would like to involve families, but many do not know how to go about building positive and productive programs and are consequently fearful about trying. This creates a "rhetoric rut," in which educators are stuck, expressing support for partnerships without taking any action.

- Just about all students at all levels—elementary, middle, and high school—want their families to be more knowledgeable partners about schooling and are willing to take active roles in assisting communications between home and school. However, students need much better information and guidance than most now receive about how their schools view partnerships and about how they can conduct important exchanges with their families about school activities, homework, and school decisions.

The research results are important because they indicate that caring communities can be built, on purpose; that they include families that might not become involved on their own; and that, by their own reports, just about all families, students, and teachers believe that partnerships are important for helping students succeed across the grades.

Good programs will look different in each site, as individual schools tailor their practices to meet the needs and interests, time and talents, and ages and grade levels of students and their families. However, there are some commonalities across successful programs at all grade levels. These include a recognition of the overlapping spheres of influence on student development; attention to various types of involvement that promote a variety of opportunities for schools, families, and communities to work together; and an Action Team for School, Family, and Community Partnerships to coordinate each school's work and progress.

Six Types of Involvement—Six Types of Caring

A framework of six major types of involvement has evolved from many studies and from many years of work by educators and families in elementary, middle, and high schools. The framework (summarized in the accompanying tables) helps educators develop more comprehensive programs of school and family partnerships and also helps researchers locate their questions and results in ways that inform and improve practice.[5]

Each type of involvement induces many different *practices* of partnership (see Table 1.1). Each type presents particular *challenges* that must be met in order to involve all families and needed *redefinitions* of some basic principles of involvement (see Table 1.2). Finally, each type is likely to lead to different *results* for students, for parents, for teaching practice, and for school climate (see Table 1.3). Thus, schools have choices about which practices will help achieve important goals. The tables provide examples of practices, challenges for successful implementation, redefinitions for up-to-date understanding, and results that have been documented and observed.

TABLE 1.1 Epstein's Framework of Six Types of Involvement for Comprehensive Programs of Partnership, and Sample Practices

Type 1 *Parenting*	Type 2 *Communicating*	Type 3 *Volunteering*	Type 4 *Learning at Home*	Type 5 *Decision Making*	Type 6 *Collaborating With Community*
Help all families establish home environments to support children as students	Design effective forms of school-to-home and home-to-school communication about school programs and their children's progress	Recruit and organize parent help and support	Provide information and ideas to families about how to help students at home with homework and other curriculum-related activities, decisions, and planning	Include parents in school decisions, developing parent leaders and representatives	Identify and integrate resources and services from the community to strengthen school programs, family practices, and student learning and development

Sample Practices

Suggestions for home conditions that support learning at each grade level	Conferences with every parent at least once a year, with follow-ups as needed	School and classroom volunteer program to help teachers, administrators, students, and other parents	Information for families on skills required for students in all subjects at each grade	Active PTA/PTO or other parent organizations, advisory councils, or committees (e.g., curriculum, safety, personnel) for parent leadership and participation	Information for students and families on community health, cultural, recreational, social support, and other programs or services
Workshops, video tapes, computerized phone messages on parenting and child rearing for each age and grade level	Language translators assist families, as needed	Parent room or family center for volunteer work, meetings, resources for families	Information on homework policies and how to monitor and discuss schoolwork at home	Independent advocacy groups to lobby and work for school reform and improvements	Information on community activities that link to learning skills and talents, including summer programs for students
Parent education and other courses or training for parents (e.g., GED, college credit, family literacy)	Weekly or monthly folders of student work sent home for review and comments	Annual postcard survey to identify all available talents, times, and locations of volunteers	Information on how to assist students to improve skills on various class and school assessments	District-level councils and committees for family and community involvement	Service integration through partnerships involving school; civic, counseling, cultural, health, recreation, and other agencies and organizations; and businesses
Family support programs to assist families with health, nutrition, and other services	Parent-student pick-up of report cards, with conferences on improving grades	Class parent, telephone tree, or other structures to provide all families with needed information	Regular schedule of homework that requires students to discuss and interact with families on what they are learning in class	Information on school or local elections for school representatives	
Home visits at transition points to preschool, elementary, middle, and high school; neighborhood meetings to help families understand schools and to help schools understand families	Regular schedule of useful notices, memos, phone calls, newsletters, and other communications	Parent patrols or other activities to aid safety and operation of school programs	Calendars with activities for parents and students to do at home or in the community	Networks to link all families with parent representatives	Service to the community by students, families, and schools (e.g., recycling, art, music, drama, and other activities for seniors or others)
	Clear information on choosing schools or courses, programs, and activities within schools		Family math, science, and reading activities at school		Participation of alumni in school programs for students
	Clear information on all school policies, programs, reforms, and transitions		Summer learning packets or activities		
			Family participation in setting student goals each year and in planning for college or work		

TABLE 1.2 Challenges and Redefinitions for the Successful Design and Implementation of the Six Types of Involvement

			Challenges		
Type 1	Type 2	Type 3	Type 4 Learning at Home	Type 5 Decision Making	Type 6 Collaborating With Community
Parenting	Communicating	Volunteering			
Provide information to all families who want it or who need it, not just to the few who can attend workshops or meetings at the school building	Review the readability, clarity, form, and frequency of all memos, notices, and other print and nonprint communications	Recruit volunteers widely so that *all* families know that their time and talents are welcome	Design and organize a regular schedule of interactive homework (e.g., weekly or bimonthly) that gives *students* responsibility for discussing important things they are learning, and helps families stay aware of the content of their children's classwork	Include parent leaders from all racial, ethnic, socioeconomic, and other groups in the school	Solve turf problems of responsibilities, funds, staff, and locations for collaborative activities
Enable families to share information about culture, background, children's talents and needs	Consider parents who do not speak English well, do not read well, or need large type	Make flexible schedules for volunteers, assemblies, and events to enable employed parents to participate	Coordinate family-linked homework activities, if students have several teachers	Offer training to enable leaders to serve as representatives of other families, with input from and return of information to all parents	Inform families of community programs for students, such as mentoring, tutoring, and business partnerships
Make sure that all information for families is clear, usable, and linked to children's success in school	Review the quality of major communications (e.g., the schedule, content, and structure of conferences; newsletters; report cards; and others)	Organize volunteer work; provide training; match time and talent with school, teacher, and student needs; and recognize efforts so that participants are productive	Involve families with their children in all important curriculum-related decisions	Include students (along with parents) in decision-making groups	Assure equity of opportunities for students and families to participate in community programs or to obtain services
	Establish clear two-way channels for communications from home to school and from school to home				Match community contributions with school goals; integrate child and family services with education

			Redefinitions		
"Workshop" to mean more than a *meeting* about a topic held at the school building at a particular time; "workshop" also may mean making information about a topic available in a variety of forms that can be viewed, heard, or read anywhere, anytime	"Communications about school programs and student progress" to mean: two-way, three-way, and many-way channels of communication that connect schools, families, students, and the community	"Volunteer" to mean anyone who supports school goals and children's learning or development in any way, at any place, and at any time—not just during the school day and at the school building	"Homework" to mean not only work done alone, but also interactive activities shared with others at home or in the community, linking schoolwork to real life	"Decision making" to mean a process of partnership, of shared views and actions toward shared goals, not just a power struggle between conflicting ideas	"Community" to mean not only the neighborhoods where students' homes and schools are located but also any neighborhoods that influence their learning and development
			"Help" at home to mean encouraging, listening, reacting, praising, guiding, monitoring, and discussing—not "teaching" school subjects	Parent "leader" to mean a real representative, with opportunities and support to hear from and communicate with other families	"Community" rated not only by low or high social or economic qualities, but by strengths and talents to support students, families, and schools
					"Community" means all who are interested in and affected by the quality of education, not just those with children in the schools

TABLE 1.3 Expected Results for Students, Parents, and Teachers of the Six Types of Involvement

Results for Students

Type 1 Parenting	Type 2 Communicating	Type 3 Volunteering	Type 4 Learning at Home	Type 5 Decision Making	Type 6 Collaborating With Community
Awareness of family supervision; respect for parents Positive personal qualities, habits, beliefs, and values, as taught by family Balance between time spent on chores, on other activities, and on homework Good or improved attendance Awareness of importance of school	Awareness of own progress and of actions needed to maintain or improve grades Understanding of school policies on behavior, attendance, and other areas of student conduct Informed decisions about courses and programs Awareness of own role in partnerships, serving as courier and communicator	Skill in communicating with adults Increased learning of skills that receive tutoring or targeted attention from volunteers Awareness of many skills, talents, occupations, and contributions of parents and other volunteers	Gains in skills, abilities, and test scores linked to homework and classwork Homework completion Positive attitude toward schoolwork View of parent as more similar to teacher, and home as more similar to school Self-concept of ability as learner	Awareness of representation of families in school decisions Understanding that student rights are protected Specific benefits linked to policies enacted by parent organizations and experienced by students	Increased skills and talents through enriched curricular and extracurricular experiences Awareness of careers and options for future education and work Specific benefits linked to programs, services, resources, and opportunities that connect students with community

Results for Parents

Understanding of and confidence about parenting, child and adolescent development, and changes in home conditions for learning as children proceed through school Awareness of own and others' challenges in parenting Feeling of support from school and other parents	Understanding school programs and policies Monitoring and awareness of child's progress Responding effectively to child's problems Interactions with teachers and ease of communications with school and teachers	Understanding teacher's job, increased comfort in school, and carryover of school activities at home Self-confidence about ability to work in school and with children, or to take steps to improve own education Awareness that families are welcome and valued at school Gains in specific skills of volunteer work	Know how to support, encourage, and help student at home each year Discussions of school, classwork, and homework Understanding of instructional program each year and of what child is learning in each subject Appreciation of teaching skills Awareness of child as a learner	Input into policies that affect child's education Feeling of ownership of school Awareness of parents' voices in school decisions Shared experiences and connections with other families Awareness of school, district, and state policies	Knowledge and use of local resources by family and child to increase skills and talents, or to obtain needed services Interactions with other families in community activities Awareness of school's role in the community, and of the community's contributions to the school

Results for Teachers

Understanding families' backgrounds, cultures, concerns, goals, needs, and views of their children Respect for families' strengths and efforts Understanding of student diversity Awareness of own skills to share information on child development	Increased diversity and use of communications with families and awareness of own ability to communicate clearly Appreciation and use of parent network for communications Increased ability to elicit and understand family views on children's programs and progress	Readiness to involve families in new ways, including those who do not volunteer at school Awareness of parent talents and interests in school and children Greater individual attention to students, with help from volunteers	Better design of homework assignments Respect of family time Recognition of equal helpfulness of single parent, dual income, and less formally educated families in motivating and reinforcing student learning Satisfaction with family involvement and support	Awareness of parent perspectives as a factor in policy development and decisions View of equal status of family representatives on committees and in leadership roles	Awareness of community resources to enrich curriculum and instruction Openness to and skill in using mentors, business partners, community volunteers, and others to assist students and augment teaching practice Knowledgeable, helpful referrals of children and families to needed services

Charting the Course

The entries in the tables are illustrative. The sample practices displayed in Table 1.1 are only a few of hundreds that may be selected or designed for each type of involvement. Although all schools may use the framework of six types as a guide, each school must chart its own course in choosing practices to meet the needs of its families and students.

The challenges shown (Table 1.2) are just a few of the many that relate to the examples. There are challenges—that is, problems—for every practice of partnerships, and they must be resolved in order to reach and engage all families in the best ways. Often, when one challenge is met, a new one will emerge.

The redefinitions (also in Table 1.2) redirect old notions so that involvement is not viewed solely as or measured only by "bodies in the building." As examples, the table calls for redefinitions of workshops, communication, volunteers, homework, decision making, and community. By redefining these familiar terms, it is possible for partnership programs to reach out in new ways to many more families.

The selected results (Table 1.3) should help correct the widespread misperception that any practice that involves families will raise children's achievement test scores. Instead, in the short term, certain practices are more likely than others to influence students' skills and scores, while other practices are more likely to affect attitudes and behaviors. Although students are the main focus of partnerships, the various types of involvement also promote various kinds of results for parents and for teachers. For example, the expected results for parents include not only leadership in decision making but also confidence about parenting, productive curriculum-related interactions with children, and many interactions with other parents and the school. The expected results for teachers include not only improved parent-teacher conferences or school-home communications but also better understanding of families, new approaches to homework, and other connections with families and the community.

Most of the results noted in Table 1.3 have been measured in at least one research study and observed as schools conduct their work. The entries are listed in positive terms to indicate the results of well-designed and well-implemented practices. It should be fully understood, however, that results may be negative if poorly designed practices exclude families or create greater barriers to communication and exchange. Research is still needed on the results of specific practices of partnership in various schools, at various grade levels, and for diverse populations of students, families, and teachers. It will be important to confirm, extend, or correct the information on results listed in Table 1.3 if schools are to make purposeful choices among practices that foster various types of involvement.

The tables cannot show the connections that occur when one practice activates several types of involvement simultaneously. For example, volunteers may organize and conduct a food bank (Type 3) that allows parents to pay $15 for $30 worth of food for their families (Type 1). The food may be subsidized by community agencies (Type 6). The recipients might then serve as volunteers for the program or in the community (perpetuating Type 3 and Type 6 activities). Consider another example. An after-school homework club run by volunteers and the community recreation department combines Type 3 and Type 6 practices. Yet it also serves as a Type 1 activity because the after-school program assists families with the supervision of their children. This practice may also alter the way homework interactions are conducted between students and parents at home (Type 4). These and other connections are interesting, and research is needed to understand the combined effects of such activities.

The tables also simplify the complex longitudinal influences that produce various results over time. For example, a series of events might play out as follows. The involvement of families in reading at home leads students to give more attention to reading and to be more strongly motivated to read. This in turn may help students maintain or improve their daily reading skills and then their reading grades. With the accumulation over time of good classroom reading programs, continued home support, and increased skills and confidence in reading, students may significantly improve their reading achievement test scores. The time between reading aloud at home and increased reading test scores may vary greatly, depending on the quality and quantity of other reading activities in school and out.

Consider yet another example. A study by Seyong Lee, using longitudinal data and rigorous statistical controls on background and prior influences, found important benefits for high school students' attitudes and grades as a result of continuing several types of family involvement from the middle school into the high school. However, achievement test scores were not greatly affected by partnerships at the high school level. Longitudinal studies and practical experiences that are monitored over time are needed to increase our understanding of the complex patterns of results that can develop from various partnership activities.[6]

The six types of involvement can guide the development of a balanced, comprehensive program of partnerships, including opportunities for family involvement at school and at home, with potentially important results for students, parents, and teachers. The results for students, parents, and teachers will depend on the particular types of involvement that are implemented as well as on the quality of the implementation.

Action Teams for School, Family, and Community Partnerships

Who will work to create caring school communities that are based on the concepts of partnership? How will the necessary work on all six types of involvement get done? Although a principal or a teacher may be a leader in working with some families or with groups in the community, one person cannot create a lasting, comprehensive program that involves all families as their children progress through the grades.

From the hard work of many educators and families in many schools, we have learned that, along with clear policies and strong support from state and district leaders and from school principals, an Action Team for School, Family, and Community Partnerships in each school is an essential structure. The action team guides the development of a comprehensive program of partnerships, including all six types of involvement, and the integration of all family and community connections within a single, unified plan and program. The trials and errors and the efforts and insights of many schools in our projects have helped identify five important steps that any school can take to develop more positive school-family-community connections.[7]

Step 1: Create an Action Team

A team approach is an appropriate way to build partnerships. The Action Team for School, Family, and Community Partnerships can be the "action arm" of a school council, if one exists. The action team takes responsibility for assessing present practices, organizing options for new partnerships, implementing selected activities, evaluating next steps, and continuing to improve and coordinate practices for all six types of involvement. Although the members of the action team lead these activities, they are assisted by other teachers, parents, students, administrators, and community members.

The action team should include at least three teachers from different grade levels, three parents with children in different grade levels, and at least one administrator. Teams may also include at least one member from the community at large and, at the middle and high school levels, at least two students from different grade levels. Others who are central to the school's work with families may also be included as members, such as a cafeteria worker, a school social worker, a counselor, or a school psychologist. Such diverse membership ensures that partnership activities will take into account the various needs, interests, and talents of teachers, parents, the school, and students.

The leader of the action team may be any member who has the respect of the other members and has good communication skills and an understanding of the partnership approach. The leader or at least one member of the action team should also serve on the school council, school improvement team, or other such body, if one exists.

In addition to group planning, members of the action team elect (or are assigned to act as) the chair or co-chair of one of six subcommittees for each type of involvement. A team with at least six members (and perhaps as many as 12) ensures that responsibilities for leadership can be delegated so that one person is not overburdened and so that the work of the action team will continue even if members move or change schools or positions. Members may serve renewable terms of two to three years, with replacement of any who leave in the interim. Other thoughtful variations in assignments and activities may be created by small or large schools using this process.

In the first phase of our work in 1987, projects were led by "project directors" (usually teachers) and were focused on one type of involvement at a time. Some schools succeeded in developing good partnerships over several years, but others were thwarted if the project director moved, if the principal changed, or if the project grew larger than one person could handle. Other schools took a team approach in order to work on many types of involvement simultaneously. Their efforts demonstrated how to structure the program for the next set of schools in our work. Starting in 1990, this second set of schools tested and improved on the structure and work of action teams. Now, all elementary, middle, and high schools in our research and development projects, and in other states and districts that are applying this work, are given assistance in taking the action team approach.

Step 2: Obtain Funds and Other Support

A modest budget is needed to guide and support the work and expenses of each school's action team. Funds for state coordinators to assist districts and schools and funds for district coordinators or facilitators to help each school may come from a number of sources. These include federal, state, and local programs that mandate, request, or support family involvement, such as Title I, Title II, Title VII, Goals 2000, and other federal and similar state funding programs. Besides paying the state and district coordinators, funds from these sources may be applied in creative ways to support staff development in the area of school, family, and community partnerships; to pay for lead teachers at each school; to set up demonstration programs; and for other partnership expenses. In addition, local school-business partnerships, school discretionary funds, and separate fund-raising efforts targeted to the schools' partnership programs have been used to support the work of their action teams. At the very least, a school's action team requires a small stipend (at least $1,000 per year for three to five years, with summer supplements) for time and materials needed by each subcommittee to plan, implement, and revise practices of partnership that include all six types of involvement.

The action team must also be given sufficient time and social support to do its work. This requires explicit support from the principal and district leaders to allow time for team members to meet, plan, and conduct the activities that are selected for each type of involvement. Time during the summer is also valuable—and may be essential—for planning new approaches that will start in the new school year.

Step 3: Identify Starting Points

Most schools have some teachers who conduct some practices of partnership with some families some of the time. How can good practices be organized and extended so that they may be used by all teachers, at all grade levels, with all families? The action team works to improve and systematize the typically haphazard patterns of involvement. It starts by collecting information about the school's present practices of partnership, along with the views, experiences, and wishes of teachers, parents, administrators, and students.

Assessments of starting points may be made in a variety of ways, depending on available resources, time, and talents. For example, the action team might use formal questionnaires[8] or telephone interviews to survey teachers, administrators, parents, and students (if resources exist to process, analyze, and report survey data). Or the action team might organize a panel of teachers, parents, and students to speak at a meeting of the parent-teacher organization or at some other school meeting as a way of initiating discussion about the goals and desired activities for partnership. Structured discussions may be conducted through a series of principal's breakfasts for representative groups of teachers, parents, students, and others; random sample phone calls may also be used to collect reactions and ideas; or formal focus groups may be convened to gather ideas about school, family, and community partnerships at the school.

What questions should be addressed? Regardless of how the information is gathered, the following areas must be covered in any information gathering:

- *Present strengths.* Which practices of school-family-community-partnerships are now working well for the school as a whole? For individual grade levels? For which types of involvement?

- *Needed changes.* Ideally, how do we want school, family, and community partnerships to work at this school three years from now? Which present practices should continue, and which should change? To reach school goals, what new practices are needed for each of the major types of involvement?

- *Expectations.* What do teachers expect of families? What do families expect of teachers and other school personnel? What do students expect their families to do to help them negotiate school life? What do students expect their teachers to do to keep their families informed and involved?

- *Sense of community.* Which families are we now reaching, and which are we not yet reaching? Who are the "hard-to-reach" families? What might be done to communicate with and engage these families in their children's education? Are current partnership practices coordinated to include all families as a school community? Or, are families whose children receive special services (e.g., Title I, special education, bilingual education) separated from other families?

- *Links to goals.* How are students faring on such measures of academic achievement as report card grades, on measures of attitudes and attendance, and on other indicators of success? How might family and community connections assist the school in helping more students reach higher goals and achieve greater success? Which practices of school, family, and community partnerships would directly connect to particular goals?

Step 4: Develop a Three-Year Plan

From the ideas and goals for partnerships collected from teachers, parents, and students, the action team can develop a three-year outline of the specific steps that will help the school progress from its starting point on each type of involvement to where it wants to be in three years. This plan outlines how each subcommittee will work over three years to make important, incremental advances to reach more families each year on each type of involvement. The three-year outline also shows how all school-family-community connections will be integrated into one coherent program of partnerships that includes activities for the whole school community, activities to meet the special needs of children and families, activities to link to the district committees and councils, and activities conducted in each grade level.

Besides the three-year outline of goals for each type of involvement, a detailed one-year plan should be developed for the first year's work. It should include the specific activities that will be implemented, improved, or maintained for each type of involvement; a timeline of monthly actions needed for each activity; identification of the subcommittee chair who will be responsible for each type of involvement; identification of the teachers, parents, students, or others (not necessarily action team members) who will assist with the implementation of each activity; indicators of how the implementation and results of each major activity will be assessed; and other details of importance to the action team.

The three-year outline and one-year detailed plan are shared with the school council and/or parent organization, with all teachers, and with the parents and students. Even if the action team makes only one good step forward each year on each of the six types of involvement, it will take 18 steps forward over three years to develop a more comprehensive and coordinated program of school-family-community partnerships.

In short, based on the input from the parents, teachers, students, and others on the school's starting points and desired partnerships, the action team will address these issues.

- *Details.* What will be done each year, for three years, to implement a program on all six types of involvement? What, specifically, will be accomplished in the first year on each type of involvement?

- *Responsibilities.* Who will be responsible for developing and implementing practices of partnership for each type of involvement? Will staff development be needed? How will teachers, administrators, parents, and students be supported and recognized for their work?

- *Costs.* What costs are associated with the improvement and maintenance of the planned activities? What sources will provide the needed funds? Will small grants or other special budgets be needed?

- *Evaluation.* How well have the practices been implemented and what are the effects on students, teachers, and families? What indicators will we use that are closely linked to the practices implemented to determine their effects?

Step 5: Continue Planning and Working

The action team should schedule an annual presentation and celebration of progress at the school so that all teachers, families, and students will know about the work that has been done each year to build partnerships. Or the district coordinator for school, family, and community partnerships might arrange an annual conference for all schools in the district. At the annual school or district meeting, the action team presents and displays the highlights of accomplishments on each type of involvement. Problems are discussed and ideas are shared about improvements, additions, and continuations for the next year.

Each year, the action team updates the school's three-year outline and develops a detailed one-year plan for the coming year's work. It is important for educators, families, students, and the community at large to be aware of annual progress, of new plans, and of how they can help.

In short, the action team addresses the following questions. How can it ensure that the program of school-family-community partnerships will continue to improve its structure, processes, and practices in order to increase the number of families who are partners with the school in their children's education? What opportunities will teachers, parents, and students have to share information on successful practices and to strengthen and maintain their efforts?

Characteristics of Successful Programs

As schools have implemented partnership programs, their experience has helped to identify some important properties of successful partnerships.

INCREMENTAL PROGRESS

Progress in partnerships is incremental, including more families each year in ways that benefit more students. Like reading or math programs, assessment programs, sports programs, or other school investments, partnership programs take time to develop, must be periodically reviewed, and should be continuously improved. The schools in our projects have shown that three years is the minimum time needed for an action team to complete a number of activities on each type of involvement and to establish its work as a productive and permanent structure in a school.

The development of a partnership is a process, not a single event. All teachers, families, students, and community groups do not engage in all activities on all types of involvement all at once. Not all activities implemented will succeed with all families. But with good planning, thoughtful implementation, well-designed activities, and pointed improvements, more and more families and teachers can learn to work with one another on behalf of the children whose interests they share. Similarly, not all students instantly improve their attitudes or achievements when their families become involved in their education. After all, student learning depends mainly on good curricula and instruction and on the work completed by students. However, with a well-implemented program of partnerships, more students will receive support from their families, and more will be motivated to work harder.

CONNECTION TO CURRICULAR AND INSTRUCTIONAL REFORM

A program of school-family-community partnerships that focuses on children's learning and development is an important component of curricular and instructional reform. Aspects of partnerships that aim to help more students succeed in school can be supported by federal, state, and local funds targeted for curricular and instructional reform. Helping families understand, monitor, and interact with students on homework, for example, can be a clear and important extension of classroom instruction as can volunteer programs that bolster and broaden student skills, talents, and interests. Improving the content and conduct of parent-teacher-student conferences and goal setting activities can be an important step in curricular reform; family support and family understanding of child and adolescent development and school curricula are necessary elements to assist students as learners.

The connection of partnerships to curriculum and instruction in schools and the location of leadership for these partnership programs in district departments of curriculum and instruction are important changes that move partnerships from being peripheral public relations activities about parents to being central programs about student learning and development.

REDEFINING STAFF DEVELOPMENT

The action team approach to partnerships guides the work of educators by restructuring "staff development" to mean colleagues working together and with parents to develop, implement, evaluate, and continue to improve practices of partnership. This is less a "dose of inservice education" than it is an active form of developing staff talents and capacities. The teachers, administrators, and others on the action team become the "experts" on this topic for their school. Their work in this area can be supported by various federal, state, and local funding programs as a clear investment in staff development for overall school reform. Indeed, the action team approach as outlined can be applied to any or all important topics on a school improvement agenda. It need not be restricted to the pursuit of successful partnerships.

It is important to note that the development of partnership programs would be easier if educators came to their schools prepared to work with families and communities. Courses or classes in preservice teacher education and in advanced degree programs are needed for teachers and administrators to help them define their professional work in terms of partnerships. Today, most educators enter schools without an understanding of family backgrounds, concepts of caring, the framework of partnerships, or the other "basics" I have discussed here. Thus, most principals and district leaders are not prepared to guide and lead their staffs in developing strong school and classroom practices that inform and involve families. And most teachers and administrators are not prepared to understand, design, implement, or evaluate good practices of partnership with the families of their students. Colleges and universities that prepare educators and others who work with children and families should identify where in their curricula the theory, research, policy, and practical ideas about partnerships are presented or where in their programs these can be added.[9]

Even with improved preservice and advanced coursework, however, each school's action team will have to tailor its menu of practices to the needs and wishes of the teachers, families, and students in the school. The framework and guidelines offered in this chapter can be used by thoughtful educators to organize this work, school by school.

The Core of Caring

One school in our Baltimore project named its partnerships the "I Care Program." It developed an I Care Patent Club that fostered fellowship and leadership of families, an *I Care Newsletter,* and many other events and activities. Other schools also gave catchy, positive names to their programs to indicate to families, students, teachers, and everyone else in the school community that there are important relationships and exchanges that must be developed to assist students.

Connection
Curricular to
Instructional and
Reform

Interestingly, synonyms for "caring" match the six types of involvement:

Type 1: *Parenting*—supporting, nurturing, and rearing

Type 2: *Communicating*—relating, reviewing, and overseeing

Type 3: *Volunteering*—supervising and fostering

Type 4: *Learning at Home*—managing, recognizing, and rewarding

Type 5: *Decision Making*—contributing, considering, and judging

Type 6: *Collaborating With the Community*—sharing and giving

Underlying all six types of involvement are two defining synonyms of caring: trusting and respecting. Of course, the varied meanings are interconnected, but it is striking that language permits us to call forth various elements of caring associated with activities for the six types of involvement. If all six types of involvement are operating well in a school's program of partnerships, then all of these caring behaviors could be activated to assist children's learning and development.

Despite real progress in many states, districts, and schools over the past few years, there are still too many schools in which educators do not understand the families of their students, in which families do not understand their children's schools, and in which communities do not understand or assist the schools, families, or students. There are still too many states and districts without the policies, departments, leadership, staff, and fiscal support needed to enable all their schools to develop good programs of partnership. Yet relatively small financial investments that support and assist the work of action teams could yield significant returns for all schools, teachers, families, and students. Educators who have led the way with trials, errors, and successes provide evidence that any state, district, or school can create similar programs.[10]

Schools have choices. There are two common approaches to involving families in schools and in their children's education. One approach emphasizes conflict and views the school as a battleground. The conditions and relationships in this kind of environment guarantee power struggles and disharmony. The other approach emphasizes partnership and views the school as a homeland. The conditions and relationships in this kind of environment invite power sharing and mutual respect and allow energies to be directed toward activities that foster student learning and development. Even when conflicts rage, however, peace must be restored sooner or later, and the partners in children's education must work together.

Next Steps: Strengthening Partnerships

Collaborative work and thoughtful give-and-take among researchers, policy leaders, educators, and parents are responsible for the progress that has been made over the past decade in understanding and developing school, family, and community partnerships. Similar collaborations will be important for future progress in this and other areas of school reform. To promote these approaches, I have established the National Network of Partnership-2000 Schools to help link state, district, and other leaders who are responsible for helping their elementary, middle, and high schools implement programs of school, family, and community partnerships by the year 2000. The state and district coordinators must be supported for at least three years by sufficient staff and budgets to enable them to help increasing numbers of elementary, middle, and high schools in their districts to plan, implement, and maintain comprehensive programs of partnership.

Partnership-2000 Schools is putting the recommendations of this chapter into practice in ways appropriate to their locations. Implementation includes applying the theory of overlapping spheres of influence, the framework of six types of involvement, and the action team approach. Researchers and staff members at Johns Hopkins University disseminate information and guidelines, send out newsletters, and hold optional annual workshops to help state and district coordinators learn new strategies and share successful ideas. Activities for leaders at the state and district levels are shared, as are school-level programs and successful partnership practices.

The National Network of Partnership-2000 Schools began its activities in fall 1995 and will continue until at least the year 2000. The goal is to enable leaders in all states and districts to assist all their schools in establishing and strengthening programs of school-family-community partnership.

Notes

1. Joyce L. Epstein, "Toward a Theory of Family-School Connections: Teacher Practices and Parent Involvement," in Klaus Hurrelmann, Frederick Kaufmann, and Frederick Losel, eds., *Social Intervention: Potential and Constraints* (New York: DeGruyter, 1987), pp. 121-136; idem, "School and Family Partnerships," in Marvin Alkin, ed., *Encyclopedia of Educational Research,* 6th ed. (New York: Macmillan, 1992), pp. 1139-1151; idem, "Theory to Practice: School and Family Partnerships Lead to School Improvement and Student Success," in Cheryl L. Fagnano and Beverly Z. Werber, eds., *School, Family and Community Interaction: A View From the Firing Lines* (Boulder, CO: Westview, 1994) pp. 39-52; and idem, *School and Family Partnerships: Preparing Educators and Improving Schools* (Boulder, CO: Westview, forthcoming).

2. Ron Brandt, "On Parents and Schools: A Conversation With Joyce Epstein," *Educational Leadership,* 1989, pp. 24-27; Epstein, "Toward a Theory"; Catherine C. Lewis, Eric Schaps, and Marilyn Watson, "Beyond the Pendulum: Creating Challenging and Caring Schools," *Phi Delta Kappan,* March 1995, pp. 547-554; and Debra Viadero, "Learning to Care," *Education Week,* October 26, 1994, pp. 31-33.

3. A. Wade Boykin, "Harvesting Culture and Talent: African American Children and Educational Reform," in Robert Rossi, ed., *Schools and Students at Risk* (New York: Teachers College Press, 1994), pp. 116-139.

4. For references to studies by many researchers, see the following literature reviews: Epstein, "School and Family Partnerships"; idem, *School and Family Partnerships*; and idem, "Perspectives and Previews on Research and Policy for School, Family, and Community Partnerships," in Alan Booth and Judith Dunn, eds., *Family-School Links: How Do They Affect Educational Outcomes?* (Hillside, NJ: Lawrence Erlbaum, 1996), pp. 209-246. Research that reports patterns of involvement across the grades, for families with low and high socioeconomic status, for one- and two-parent homes, and on schools' programs of partnership includes Carol Ames with Madhab Khoju and Thomas Watkins, "Parents and Schools: The Impact of School-to-Home Communications on Parents' Beliefs and Perceptions," Center on Families, Communities, Schools and Children's Learning, Center Report 15, Johns Hopkins University, 1993; David P. Baker and David L. Stevenson, "Mothers' Strategies for Children's School Achievement: Managing the Transition to High School," *Sociology of Education,* vol. 59, 1986, pp. 156-166; Patricia A. Bauch, "Is Parent Involvement Different in Private Schools?" *Educational Horizons,* vol. 66, 1988, pp. 78-82; Henry J. Becker and Joyce L. Epstein, "Parent Involvement: A Study of Teacher Practices," *The Elementary School Journal,* vol. 83, 1982, pp. 85-102; Reginald M. Clark, *Family Life and School Achievement: Why Poor Black Children Succeed or Fail* (Chicago: University of Chicago Press, 1983); Susan L. Dauber and Joyce L. Epstein, "Parents' Attitudes and Practices of Involvement in Inner-City Elementary and Middle Schools," in Nancy Chavkin, ed., *Families and Schools in a Pluralistic Society* (Albany: State University of New York Press, 1993), pp. 53-71; Sanford M. Dornbusch and Philip L. Ritter, "Parents of High School Students: A Neglected Resource," *Educational Horizons,* vol. 66, 1988, pp. 75-77; Jacquelynne S. Eccles, "Family Involvement in Children's and Adolescents' Schooling," in Booth and Dunn, op. cit.; Joyce L. Epstein, "Parents' Reactions to Teacher Practices of Parent Involvement," *The Elementary School Journal,* vol. 86, 1986, pp. 277-294; idem, "Single Parents and the Schools: Effects of Marital Status on Parent and Teacher Interactions," in Maureen Hallinan, ed., *Change in Societal Institutions* (New York: Plenum, 1990), pp. 91-121; Joyce L. Epstein and Seyong Lee, "National Patterns of School and Family Connections in the Middle Grades," in Bruce A. Ryan and Gerald R. Adams, eds., *The Family-School Connection: Theory, Research and Practice* (Thousand Oaks, CA: Sage, 1995), pp. 108-154; Annette Lareau, *Home Advantage: Social Class and Parental Intervention in Elementary Edu-*

cation (Philadelphia: Falmer, 1989); and Diane Scott-Jones, "Activities in the Home That Support School Learning in the Middle Grades," in Barry Rutherford, ed., *Creating Family / School Partnerships* (Columbus, OH: National Middle School Association, 1995), pp. 161-181.

5. The three tables update earlier versions that were based on only five types of involvement. For other discussions on the types, practices, challenges, redefinitions, and results, see Epstein, "School and Family Partnerships"; Lori J. Connors and Joyce L. Epstein, "Parents and Schools," in Marc H. Bornstein, ed., *Handbook of Parenting* (Hillsdale, NJ: Lawrence Erlbaum, 1995), pp. 437-458; Joyce L. Epstein and Lori J. Connors, "School and Family Partnerships in the Middle Grades," in Barry Rutherford, op. cit.; and idem, "Trust Fund: School, Family, and Community Partnerships in High Schools," Center on Families, Communities, Schools and Children's Learning, Center Report 24, Johns Hopkins University, 1994. Schools' activities with various types of involvement are outlined in Don Davies, Patricia Burch, and Vivian Johnson, "A Portrait of Schools Reaching Out: Report of a Survey on Practices and Policies of Family-Community-School Collaboration," Center on Families, Communities, Schools and Children's Learning, Center Report 1, Johns Hopkins University, 1992.

6. Seyong Lee, *Family-School Connections and Students' Education: Continuity and Change of Family Involvement from the Middle Grades to High School* (doctoral diss., Johns Hopkins University, 1994). For a discussion of issues concerning the results of partnerships, see Epstein, "Perspectives and Previews." For various research reports on results of partnerships for students and for parents, see Joyce L. Epstein, "Effects on Student Achievement of Teacher Practices of Parent Involvement," in Steven Silvern, ed., *Literacy Through Family, Community, and School Interaction* (Greenwich, CT: JAI, 1991), pp. 261-276; Joyce L. Epstein and Susan L. Dauber, "Effects on Students of an Interdisciplinary Program Linking Social Studies, Art, and Family Volunteers in the Middle Grades," *Journal of Early Adolescence,* vol. 15, 1995, pp. 237-266; Joyce L. Epstein and Jill Jacobsen, "Effects of School Practices to Involve Families in the Middle Grades: Parents' Perspectives" (paper presented at the annual meeting of the American Sociological Association, Los Angeles, August 1994); Joyce L. Epstein and Seyong Lee, "Effects of School Practices to Involve Families on Parents and Students in the Middle Grades: A View from the Schools" (paper presented at the annual meeting of the American Sociological Association, August 1993); and Anne T. Henderson and Nancy Berla, *A New Generation of Evidence: The Family Is Critical to Student Achievement* (Washington, DC: National Committee for Citizens in Education, 1994).

7. Lori J. Connors and Joyce L. Epstein, "Taking Stock: The Views of Teachers, Parents, and Students on School, Family, and Community Partnerships in High Schools," Center on Families, Communities, Schools and Children's Learning, Center Report 25, Johns Hopkins University, 1994; Epstein and Connors, "Trust Fund"; Joyce L. Epstein and Susan L. Dauber, "School Programs and Teacher Practices of Parent Involvement in Inner-City Elementary and Middle Schools," *Elementary School Journal,* vol. 91, 1991, pp. 289-303; and Joyce L. Epstein,

Susan C. Herrick, and Lucretia Coates, "Effects of Summer Home
Learning Packets on Student Achievement in Language Arts in the
Middle Grades," *School Effectiveness and School Improvement,* forth-
coming. For other approaches to action teams for partnerships, see Pa-
tricia Burch and Ameetha Palanki, "Action Research on Family-School-
Community Partnerships," *Journal of Emotional and Behavioral
Problems,* vol. 1, 1994, pp. 16-19; Patricia Burch, Ameetha Palanki, and
Don Davies, "In Our Hands: A Multi-Site Parent-Teacher Action Re-
search Project," Center on Families, Communities, Schools and Chil-
dren's Learning, Center Report 29, Johns Hopkins University, 1995;
Don Davies, "Schools Reaching Out: Family, School and Community
Partnerships for Students' Success," *Phi Delta Kappan,* vol. 72, 1991,
pp. 376-382; idem, "A More Distant Mirror: Progress Report on a Cross-
National Project to Study Family-School-Community Partnerships,"
Equity and Choice, vol. 19, 1993, pp. 41-46; and Don Davies, Ameetha
Palanki, and Patricia Burch, "Getting Started: Action Research in Fam-
ily-School-Community Partnerships," Center on Families, Communi-
ties, Schools and Children's Learning, Center Report 17, Johns Hopkins
University, 1993. For an example of an organizing mechanism for ac-
tion teams, see Vivian R. Johnson, "Parent Centers in Urban Schools:
Four Case Studies," Center on Families, Communities, Schools and
Children's Learning, Center Report 23, Johns Hopkins University, 1994.

8. Surveys for teachers and parents in the elementary and middle grades and for teachers, parents, and students in high school, developed and revised in 1993 by Joyce L. Epstein, Karen Clark Salinas,
and Lori J. Connors, are available from the Center on School, Family,
and Community Partnerships at Johns Hopkins University.

9. Mary Sue Ammon, "University of California Project on
Teacher Preparation for Parent Involvement, Report I: April 1989 Conference and Initial Follow-up," mimeo, University of California,
Berkeley, 1990; Nancy F. Chavkin and David L. Williams, "Critical Issues in Teacher Training for Parent Involvement," *Educational Horizons,* vol. 66, 1988, pp. 87-89; and Lisa Hinz, Jessica Clarke, and Joe
Nathan, "A Survey of Parent Involvement Course Offerings in Minnesota's Undergraduate Preparation Programs," Center for School
Change, Humphrey Institute of Public Affairs, University of Minnesota, Minneapolis, 1992. To correct these deficiencies in the education
of educators, I have written a course text or supplementary reader
based on the theory, framework, and approaches described in this chapter; see Epstein, *School and Family Partnerships.* Other useful read-
ings for a university course include Sandra L. Christenson and Jane
Close Conoley, eds., *Home-School Collaboration: Enhancing Children's
Academic Competence* (Silver Spring, MD: National Association of
School Psychologists, 1992); Fagnano and Werber, op. cit.; Norman
Fruchter, Anne Galletta, and J. Lynne White, *New Directions in Parent
Involvement* (Washington, DC: Academy for Educational Development,
1992); William Rioux and Nancy Berla, eds., *Innovations in Parent and
Family Involvement* (Princeton Junction, NJ: Eye on Education, 1993);
and Susan McAllister Swap, *Developing Home-School Partnerships:
From Concepts to Practice* (New York: Teachers College Press, 1993).

10. See, for example, Gary Lloyd, "Research and Practical Application for School, Family, and Community Partnerships," in Booth and Dunn, op. cit.; Wisconsin Department of Public Instruction, *Sharesheet: The DPI Family-Community School Partnership Newsletter,* August/September 1994; and the special section on parent involvement in the January 1991 *Phi Delta Kappan.*

2

_____

Using the Framework in Practice

Stories From the Field

Baltimore's Story: Finding the Keys to School, Family, and Community Partnerships

Lucretia Coates, Baltimore City Public Schools

This section describes how the framework of six types of involvement and the Action Team approach described in Chapter 1 are implemented in schools in Baltimore. The author, Lucretia Coates, served for eight years as the Field Director for the Baltimore School, Family, and Community Connections Project. From 1987 to 1995, Ms. Coates was a teacher on leave of absence from the Baltimore City Public Schools, working with the Fund for Educational Excellence and Johns Hopkins University. She helped design the project and assisted a set of pilot schools, replication sites, and all elementary and middle schools in one region of the city to implement and improve school-family-community connections. Working together, researchers and educators learned about good practices and successful strategies that can help all schools develop more comprehensive programs of partnership. Here, Lucretia Coates describes the "keys" that open doors to effective partnerships, and how district leadership can help schools conduct this work.

School Stories: Examples of the Six Types of Involvement

Reporters: Charlene Bratton, Gita Lefstein, Lucretia Coates, Adele Israel, Paula Williams, and Jackie Griswold, Baltimore City Public Schools

Educators who were members of Action Teams for School, Family, and Community Partnerships share examples of successful practices for each of the six types of involvement. The six reports of helpful prac-

26

tices illustrate a few of the hundreds of ways that schools can reach out to more and more families. These ideas can be adopted or adapted to the special needs or circumstances in other elementary, middle, and high schools. The sample practices are not necessarily the best or only effective practices for each type of involvement. They are examples of reasonable and useful activities.

Baltimore's Story: Finding the Keys to School, Family, and Community Partnerships

Lucretia Coates, Baltimore City Public Schools

Have you ever misplaced your house keys or your car keys? Pretty frustrating! Many educators, parents, and community members have experienced a similar frustration in their attempts to open doors to increase the participation and involvement of all who care about and influence students. Many studies indicate that family and community involvement are important for children's success in school. However, when educators look closely at how they reach out to families, most realize that there is room for improvement in their schools.

In Baltimore, teachers, administrators, parents, and students have worked for several years to identify the "keys" that will open doors to school-family-community partnerships. Our joint program is sponsored by the Fund for Educational Excellence (FUND), the Johns Hopkins University Center on School, Family, and Community Partnerships, and the Baltimore City Public Schools. The program has grown and participants have learned a lot because of the work we have done together and because of the energy and efforts of many teachers, parents, students, principals, and community partners.

The Keys to Partnerships: Epstein's Six Types of Involvement

Some schools interpret successful parental involvement as the number of parent volunteers at school. Others interpret involvement as the number of parents who attend parent-teacher conferences. Still other schools interpret a lack of parent participation or low attendance at meetings as an indication of parental disinterest in the school and disregard for their children. Schools participating in the Baltimore School, Family, and Community Connections Project soon realized that each of these interpretations represents too narrow a vision of parental involvement.

Joyce Epstein's framework of six types of involvement, based on many studies including some in our Baltimore project schools, provides a broader vision of involvement that includes all families at all grades. After many trials and errors, tests, and improvements in over 50 schools, the framework now can be applied with confidence by any school that wants to improve its partnerships with all families and groups in the community.

Using the Keys to Open Your School's Doors to Partnerships

For the six keys to fit your school's doors to partnership, everyone must take responsibility for needed actions. One administrator, or one teacher, or one family coordinator cannot build a strong program. All of the school staff, all families, and the students must understand the goals for partnership and do their part to reach those goals. Schools must see that involving families is not an additional or separate program but part of the school's *total* program—part of the school's regular work. Strategies and practices to encourage all six types of involvement must be implemented to help the school and students reach the goals set in the school improvement plan or other important goals.

Creating the Action Team

The job of building a comprehensive program of school, family, and community partnerships is too big for any one person to do alone. Most schools already have a social committee or a curriculum committee to coordinate activities. Similarly, a team of teachers, parents, administrators, and others is needed to serve as the nucleus for planning, implementing, and evaluating the school-family-community partnership program. This group is the Action Team for School, Family, and Community Partnerships. It works to ensure that the six types of involvement are implemented in ways that help reach school goals for students, improve school climate, and engage families in their children's education.

It is important that members of the Action Team for School, Family, and Community Partnerships understand the team's tasks, roles, and responsibilities. It also is important that other staff and all parents and students know about the existence and work of the Action Team. Everyone needs to know what goals for school improvement have been set, and that the school has a program of partnerships to help reach those goals. The Action Team for School, Family, and Community Partnerships can help disseminate this information, and involve all families and their communities in children's education at school, at home, and in many locations in the community.

The Keys to Planning and Implementing A Partnership Program at Your School

Successful plans start with plans for success. Failing to plan ensures that programs will fail. Strong family, school, and community partnerships do not happen overnight, but they can be developed with good work over time.

The first task for the Action Team is to identify the school's present strengths and weaknesses in each of the six types of involvement. Then, decisions must be made about which practices to keep, which to change, and which to add to create a comprehensive, balanced program of partnerships and to achieve important goals.

Each Action Team creates a three-year outline and a one-year action plan. The members must be realistic about what can be accomplished in one year and consider annually how to build on their program of school-family-community partnerships. Each year, the three-year outline is revised and a new one-year action plan is designed to continually increase the number of families involved and improve the quality of activities for family and community participation.

Regularly scheduled messages from the principal also help keep the program of school-family-community partnerships on everyone's agenda. These messages must reinforce that partnerships are a vital part of the school's program, highlight important activities that the Action Team and others are implementing, and welcome the participation of all families in these activities.

Monitoring Results

As practices are implemented, schools should determine if and how the activities benefit students, parents, staff, and/or the school. The Action Team may use short surveys, interviews, sign-in sheets, and comparisons of participation "before and after" practices are implemented to assess the results or the effects of particular practices. Even if these evaluations are relatively informal, it is important to learn how each practice is working to inform future plans and improvements.

It is important to be realistic about the *results* of particular practices. For example, it is unrealistic to believe that having a Mother and Daughter Banquet or Father and Son Breakfast will improve math or reading skills. Realistically, these important gatherings of children with their guests help families feel more welcome at the school and might present families with information about the school's math or reading program. Having information, however, is just one small part of helping students do better in school subjects. Therefore, a banquet may help a school reach its goal to become a more welcoming place, but more will be needed in the daily lessons by teachers in class and in regular interactions of families and students at home to help students improve math (or other) skills.

Key Challenges for Program Implementation

In the real world of schools and classrooms, teachers and administrators often feel that they are already on "overload" and that they do not have the time to become involved in yet another committee. These days, most schools do not have money for new initiatives. These are real challenges. It is important that schools see the Action Team for School, Family, and Community Partnerships as part of their regular work. If there are too many committees, then some related committees might need to be incorporated into the Action Team to ensure that connections with families are activated to help reach school goals. It also is important that the Action Team has time to do its work; otherwise, it will be a committee without a chance for success. Some of the ways our schools have made time to plan and work are the following:

- Schedule resource classes, elective or enrichment classes, planning periods, or lunch periods of the teachers on the Action Team at the same time so that all members have the same time periods to meet together to report and plan their work.

- Recruit parent volunteers to provide class coverage for an hour or so while teachers meet. In some schools, the program for volunteers includes training parents or other family members to assist the staff in this way.

- Find funds to support the Action Team's work during the summer, or to pay for substitute teachers for half days during the school year, provide transportation, fares, and child care for parents on the Action Team, or arrange other schedules and support to ensure that all teachers, administrators, and parents on the Action Team are free to meet together at the same time.

- Readjust the school day. Extend the instructional day four days of the week and release students early on one day. This provides one afternoon each week for staff development and for the Action Team and other committees to meet, plan, and do the work needed to improve the school program and chances for student success.

Securing funds for program costs for improving school-family-community partnerships may be simply a matter of examining how best to use dollars that already have been allocated for staff development or family involvement. In our program, schools could apply for small grants from the FUND, a local education foundation supporting innovation and improvement in the public schools. One participating school held a candy drive with all profits going to the Action Team for School, Family, and Community Partnerships' program to increase family and community involvement.

The keys to implementing a successful school program include these:

- Create an Action Team for School, Family, and Community Partnerships.

- Provide training for the Action Team so that all members understand the process of building a comprehensive program of partnerships.

- Provide information to the full staff and all families about the goals and work of the Action Team and the agenda for school improvement.

- Enable the Action Team to do the following:

  1. Assess the school's present strengths and weaknesses on each of the six types of involvement.

2. Develop a three-year outline and a one-year action plan that link the activities for partnership with the school's goals for students.

3. Enlist other staff, parents, and groups in the community (businesses, agencies, museums, and others) to help design, implement, and evaluate the results of the activities on each year's plan for partnerships.

4. Arrange an annual celebration and report of progress to inform everyone of the progress made in improving partnerships and to gather ideas for improvements for next year's plan.

Making the "Connection" at the District Level

Goals 2000 legislation names school, family, and community partnerships as one of the eight national goals for all schools. Title I legislation specifies and mandates programs and practices of school, family, and community partnerships in order to qualify for and maintain funding. Many states, districts, and schools are writing and implementing policies to guide schools in creating more systemic connections with families and communities.

School districts must do more than say that parents are welcome in district planning and school programs. Central offices must take the lead by setting policies that demonstrate that family involvement is a priority for every school. Many schools place importance on the guidelines and evaluations from their central office. For example, if standardized tests in reading, math, writing, and other subject areas are administered and used by the central office to reward or recognize schools, most schools will work to prepare their students to perform as well as possible on the tests.

If the central office evaluates and recognizes good school-family-community partnerships, most schools will work to improve and maintain family involvement.

There are many forms that district leadership might take. In our Baltimore project, schools were assisted by facilitators who worked with the local community foundation, the FUND. They performed the district-level functions of guiding Action Teams, assisting them with their work, conducting school-site and multi-school cluster meetings, and holding annual conferences for sharing ideas, progress, and new plans. In recent years, Area Assistant Superintendents in Baltimore have shown how, in large, urban systems, district-level leadership can be provided by the administrators of large numbers of schools in geographic regions of the city.

The communications and support from district leaders are extra "keys" that open school doors to partnerships. One Area Superintendent in Baltimore acknowledged every school's Action Team chairperson by writing a personal letter of thanks. In his monthly meetings for principals, this Area Superintendent included on the agenda a "spotlight" on school, family, and community partnerships. One or two principals would share their school's progress in building school, family, and community partnerships with their colleagues. He also included principals' leadership and support for their schools' Action Teams among the criteria for principals' annual evaluations. The message to principals from this district leader was clear: I am holding you responsible for developing good school-family-community connections in your school.

To demonstrate that family involvement is a priority, a school district should consider these actions:

- *Identify clear and definitive goals for family and school partnerships.* These goals should be stated clearly in the district's mission statement.

- *Incorporate criteria for strong partnerships into the evaluations of administrators and teachers.*

- *Establish an Office for School, Family, and Community Partnerships.* A district-level office with a leader and adequate staff and support should be identified as the place that will assist schools in their efforts to develop and build comprehensive programs of school, family, and community partnerships. This office would do the following:

  1. Provide staff training for schools to help them plan and implement comprehensive programs of partnership.

  2. Provide ongoing technical support to schools to help them evaluate their work and continue to develop their program over time.

  3. Monitor schools' progress.

  4. Provide opportunities for schools to network with other schools to share ideas.

  5. Build expertise within each school to maintain strong partnerships as part of the regular school program.

District leadership is crucial for all schools to have strong programs of school-family-community partnerships. Action Teams for School, Family, and Community Partnerships are crucial in each school in order to create programs that are tailored to the needs and goals of the school. Together, district and school activities provide the keys that open doors to partnerships.

School Stories

EXAMPLES OF THE SIX TYPES OF INVOLVEMENT

Type 1: Parenting

Type 1 activities increase families' understanding of their children as students. This includes assisting parents with information on children's health, safety, nutrition, other topics of child and adolescent development, and home conditions that support education at each grade level.

Type 1 activities also increase schools' understanding of families. This requires strategies that promote exchanges of information between schools and families about their care and concerns for children.

Parents play a key role in helping students get to school on time every day. Schools can help families understand this parenting responsibility and can work together with families to improve or maintain students' school attendance.

One example of an effective Type 1 activity is an "Attendance Summit" that has been held at a Baltimore City elementary school since 1991. Charlene Bratton, a master teacher at the school, reports the development, implementation, and results of the school's Attendance Summit.

Her summary explains the collaborative efforts of educators, parents, and others in the community. Their collective awareness, creativity, and commitment to improving student attendance and family involvement has ensured the success of this Type 1 activity.

Sample Type 1 Activity

ATTENDANCE SUMMIT

Reporter: Charlene Bratton, Master Teacher

We designed our Attendance Summit to respond to ideas gathered from parents and teachers about how to improve attendance. We gave special attention to the concerns and needs of families whose students have particularly poor attendance.

At the Summit many kinds of information were shared. Groups of parents rotated every fifteen minutes to hear the various presenters. A question and answer period was conducted in each session after information was distributed and discussed.

The school system provided a speaker and literature to explain the legal issues about student attendance and family responsibilities. This information was particularly helpful to case managers and parents. A school nurse identified health resources that parents could contact when their children were ill. Teachers shared information with parents about the importance of education and how attendance affected children's academic programs and their chances for success.

Another speaker helped parents devise morning schedules for their children and themselves to ensure that children arrive at school on time. Community groups provided calendars, pencils, and stickers that parents could use as rewards and incentives to encourage their children to follow scheduled times for wake-up, leaving for school, homework, chores, play, bedtime, and other activities. Alarm clocks were also given to families who needed them.

We used several communication strategies to invite parents to the Attendance Summit including letters, phone calls, and parent-to-parent communications. The Attendance Summit was scheduled in the evening to give parents ample time to return home from work, prepare dinner, and conduct other daily activities. Baby-sitting services were provided for parents who needed child care in order to attend. Refreshments and activities were provided for children.

The first Attendance Summit was successful and now is an annual activity at the school. Since its inception, our students have progressively improved their attendance. In 1991, the school was not meeting the State's standard for a "satisfactory" rating. The attendance rate for pre-k through fifth grade was only 90.6%. As of June 1995, attendance reached 93.5%, just 0.5% away from a satisfactory attendance rating.

We are continuing to encourage students and parents to pay attention to attendance through monthly, quarterly, and yearly activities. Parents know whom to contact if a student has a prolonged illness or if a family situation arises that requires a child to stay home from school. Students with improved, good, and excellent attendance are recognized. Movies, treats, certificates, and other acknowledgments are provided for the students.

The Attendance Summit makes it possible to systematically involve families in an essential conversation about attendance policies and parents' roles in supporting those policies. The Summit is supported by other activities that keep students aware and proud of good attendance at school. We are aiming to attain 97% attendance and an "excellent" rating for the school.

School Stories

EXAMPLES OF THE SIX TYPES OF INVOLVEMENT

Type 2: Communicating

Type 2 activities include school-to-home and home-to-school communications about school and classroom programs and children's progress. Two-way communications by teachers and families increase understanding and cooperation between school and home. Thoughtful and frequent communications show students that their teachers and parents are working together to help students succeed in school.

Many Type 2 activities are used in schools to increase two-way communications including parent-teacher conferences, phone calls, homework hotlines, newsletters with reaction sheets, report card pick-ups, half-and-half memos, and other creative strategies. Two-way communications encourage families to provide reactions, ideas, preferences, and questions about school programs and children's progress.

One example of an effective Type 2 activity is a series called "Family Fun and Learning Nights." These monthly evening programs were developed by one Baltimore City elementary school to generate a sense of community, help families understand school programs, motivate students to learn, give parents ideas and tools for extending learning at home, and provide parents, teachers, administrators, and students with opportunities to interact informally at school.

Teacher Gita Lefstein describes "Family Fun and Learning Nights," sharing her insights on the successful implementation of these programs. Many schools conduct variations of family fun nights, usually once or twice a year, to provide information about school programs and to strengthen the base for two-way communications between home and school.

Sample Type 2 Activity

FAMILY FUN AND LEARNING NIGHTS

Reporter: Gita Lefstein, Teacher

Our Family Fun and Learning Nights usually are scheduled for two hours. For the first hour to hour and a half, students and parents participate together in a variety of fun activities under the supervision of a teacher. For example, one science activity asks parents and students to work together to construct insulators and test which insulators keep an ice cube from melting for the longest time. A math activity places parents and students in cooperative groups to figure out different ways of making 81 cents with five coins. Parents also are provided with suggestions for continuing the activities or other fun learning activities they can do at home.

Following the activities, parents and older students fill out evaluations to help us improve the next Family Fun and Learning Night. Then everyone shares in a light meal. This gives parents and teachers a chance to meet and talk together in an informal setting.

Is it worth it? Over 200 parents and students attended some of the monthly sessions for food, fun, and information about learning. There was high support from the teachers, administrators, and other staff. The following quotations from some of the parents' evaluation sheets speak for themselves:

> "I loved today and it was great!"

> "I plan to try more bubble experiments at home, even with my 20-month old."

> "I did something new and I plan to buy my grandchildren pattern toys."

> "I think the fun night was very educational and all schools should have activities such as these."

> "I think that this is a great activity for the kids and parents. It helps you to learn what the children are doing in their classes."

One potential problem for some schools is the burn-out that may occur if only a few staff members carry the load to make all of the arrangements for a Family Fun and Learning Night. In our school, we did not have this problem. We recruited volunteers from full-time and part-time staff—substitutes, aides, custodians, resource teachers, and others—to invite families and conduct the activities. We divided the responsibilities and the work. We didn't ask the same people to assist or attend every month. The success of the first Family Fun and Learning Night created enthusiasm that helped bring out staff and families for the other evenings.

School Stories

EXAMPLES OF THE SIX TYPES OF INVOLVEMENT

Type 3: Volunteering

Type 3 activities enable families to give their time and talents to support schools, teachers, and children. Family volunteers assist individual teachers or help in the library, family center, computer room, playground, lunchroom, or other locations. Volunteers may conduct activities at school, at home, or in the community.

Families also give their time to attend student performances, games, assemblies, celebrations, or other events. Their presence in schools as volunteers or as audiences not only strengthens school programs, but also communicates to students, faculty, and the community that parents care about the quality of their schools and are willing to help children reach important school goals.

Various strategies are used to recruit and train volunteers and match their time and talents to the needs of teachers, students, and administrators. Schools also must decide how to schedule opportunities so that all families can volunteer and attend events even if they work during the school day.

Educators in one Baltimore City elementary school explained, "Many of our parents are available to assist and volunteer at school, but we only get the same two or three parents." This is a familiar complaint in many schools. The school's Action Team worked with Field Director Lucretia Coates (now a principal) to answer the question: How shall we get more parents to volunteer at school?

They initiated a Parent Club to encourage and organize parent volunteers. Ms. Coates describes the features of the Parent Club that gives families a place to meet, talk, and work with each other, and to organize and conduct volunteer activities.

Sample Type 3 Activity

PARENT CLUB
Reporter: Lucretia Coates, Principal

A Parent Club brings families together in a friendly environment where they feel welcomed and valued. It also may be called a Family Center, Family Resource Room, Parent Room, or another name to designate a place in the school for parents to meet and assist the school, teachers, children, and other families. Volunteers can work in the Parent Club room, or they may be requested to come to classrooms or other school locations. The room may serve as the volunteers' home-base at school.

A Parent Club is not a formal Parent Teacher Association (P.T.A.) or Parent Teacher Organization (P.T.O.). These groups are usually more involved in school policies and decision making. In schools that do not have formal parent associations or have not yet added parents to their Advisory Councils or School Improvement Teams, a Parent Club may serve as a first step in preparing parents to take leadership roles in the school.

A Parent Club must have a leader/advisor/coordinator who serves as a link between home and school. This may be a parent liaison, counselor, teacher, assistant principal, community resource person, or other talented individual. The leader is responsible for recruiting members, setting the tone of Parent Club meetings, and helping parents feel at ease in the school. The leader must be sensitive to the differences in backgrounds, interests, skills, and talents of parents in order to help all families become contributing members of the Parent Club and helpful volunteers. The leader cannot dominate, but must be able to foster an atmosphere in which everyone feels vital and necessary. The leader conducts regularly scheduled meetings (at least once a week), helps organize activities, and coordinates teachers' requests for volunteers with parents' available time and talents.

Another key player in the organization and success of a Parent Club is the school principal. As an educational leader, the principal is responsible for welcoming parents, helping teachers and school staff understand the importance of parent participation, and encouraging parents to become involved in the Parent Club and other activities. The principal must designate a room for the Parent Club and support the meetings and activities conducted by the Parent Club.

Once parents are active partners, they soon find many ways to assist the school. In this elementary school, Parent Club members were asked to volunteer for a parent-child reading program, assist with a computer drive sponsored by a local grocery store, and assist the school, teachers, children, and administrators in other ways. During Black History month, the Parent Club organized an African Food Tasting Party. They researched African food, served food to students, and provided background information to teachers. They also learned other leadership roles. For example, for the first time, they went to lobby legislators at the state capital for increased education funding.

Although only a few parents attended the first meeting of the Parent Club, almost thirty participated by the end of the school year. When parents feel that they are contributing and needed partners, they become the Club's best recruiters for more volunteers. As a school builds a full program of partnerships, the Parent Club room may serve as a place where many types of involvement activities are conducted in addition to volunteer work.

School Stories

EXAMPLES OF THE SIX TYPES OF INVOLVEMENT

Type 4: Learning at Home

Type 4 activities provide information and ideas to families about the academic work their children do in class, how to help their children with homework, and other curriculum-related activities and decisions. Type 4 activities increase family discussions about academic work.

In all of these activities, students are key participants because learning and homework are their responsibilities, and decisions about courses, programs, and future plans affect their lives. Strategies such as interactive homework are used to encourage students to share interesting work and skills they are learning in class with their families. These activities encourage families to link their own knowledge and everyday experiences to students' schoolwork.

There are a number of ways to involve families with students on curricular issues. One example of a successful learning-at-home initiative is the Read With Me Program, described by retired educator and current parent-community coordinator, Adele Israel. This project, implemented in a Baltimore City elementary school, combines the work of volunteers (Type 3) at school with the involvement of all parents and children learning at home (Type 4), illustrating the power of combining types of involvement to reach a school goal—improved attitudes and experiences in reading.

There are many variations of shared reading in which enjoyable books, tapes, puppets, and other materials are sent home in colorful, sturdy bags or boxes to help children and parents read together and discuss ideas about fiction, non-fiction, poems, plays, and themes. In all shared reading programs, the goals are to enable families to help children strengthen their reading skills and increase their love of reading.

Sample Type 4 Activity

THE "READ WITH ME" PROGRAM

Reporter: Adele Israel, Parent-Community Coordinator

The Read With Me Program is based on the assumption that more students will succeed in school if their parents take an active role in helping them to work hard and enjoy learning. This program involves a parent or another family member at home as a "reading buddy" with the student. It shows that a parent does not have to be in the school building to be involved in their child's education. Parents read with the child to encourage regular reading habits and to help the child find pleasure in reading good books. It also lets children know that their parents are interested in their education, and that reading can be a shared activity.

The Read With Me Carry Home Library includes a book and a cassette tape of the same story in a colorful canvas carry-bag. The books and tapes are children's favorites by award-winning authors, suitable for each grade level. An activity sheet is included with easy-to-read questions about the story that parents and children discuss at home. The completed activity sheet is signed by the family member who reads with the child and is returned with the other materials in the bag. The activity sheets serve as a record of the number of books read by each child, the person who shared the reading activity, and comments made by the parent or other "reading buddy."

Three short training sessions are held for parent volunteers or class parents from each classroom. In the first session, parents are shown the materials included in the kits. They also set up the Read With Me Library on a shelf in the Parent Room. In the next session, parents discuss borrowing procedures and are given folders to guide them with this work. In the third training session, the Parent Coordinator instructs the class parents about how to complete the borrowing forms and how to prepare the materials to send home with the students.

Students may borrow a different book each week during the school year. In this program, about seventy-five bags of books, tapes, and activity/discussion sheets were prepared for each classroom. The books were ordered from a company that offers children's books for each grade level at reasonable rates. It takes some work to start this program, but the materials can be used for several years by many children and families.

In the first two years of the program, three kindergarten and three first grade classes were involved. To acquaint students with the Read With Me Program, the Principal and Parent Coordinator invited participating classes and parents to the school auditorium for a kick-off program. Colorful posters were hung around the school building showing a Read With Me logo. The books, tapes, activity sheets, and bags were shown and discussed. In the first year of the program, over 800 activity sheets were completed, indicating high family involvement. In the second year, even more family members participated.

EXAMPLES OF THE SIX TYPES OF INVOLVEMENT

Type 5: Decision Making

Type 5 activities enable families to participate in decisions about school programs that affect their own and other children. Family representatives on school councils, school improvement teams, committees, and in the PTA, PTO, or other parent organizations ensure that parents' voices are heard on school decisions.

Whether they serve in leadership roles or not, all families need good information about school and district policies, and must have opportunities to offer ideas, perspectives, and reactions to improve the quality of their schools and programs. When parent representatives do their jobs well, they gather ideas and return information to the families they represent. Type 5 activities increase parental awareness of how the school and school system work, and increase feelings of ownership of the school.

Paula Williams, a Baltimore City elementary school teacher (now a program facilitator), found that by establishing a School Action Team (SAT) that worked closely with the School Improvement Team (SIT), her school became more democratic and effective. Her report indicates that the SAT takes account of perspectives and concerns of teachers, students, parents, and community members, and takes action to improve school-family connections and other school goals.

An Action Team for School, Family, and Community Partnerships is the basic structure that helps schools develop strong programs of partnership. As in many places, Ms. Williams' school gave the team its own name—the School Action Team (SAT). Her report illustrates how each Action Team for Partnerships tailors its work to support the school's goals.

Sample Type 5 Activity

THE SCHOOL ACTION TEAM

Reporter: Paula Williams, Program Facilitator

The School Action Team (SAT) is responsible for implementing a comprehensive approach to school, family, and community partnerships. The team consists of grade-level teachers, parents, students, a parent liaison, an administrator, a master teacher, a representative from the special education department, a representative from the PTA/PTO organization, and representatives from the community. Thus, many stakeholders in our children's education serve on the team.

The Chairperson of the SAT is a member of our School Improvement Team (SIT). In our school, the School Action Team creates subcommittees for each of the goals set by the School Improvement Team. The subcommittees select activities from the six types of involvement to help meet each goal. By mobilizing school, family, and community resources, we have a better chance of solving problems and reaching our goals to improve attendance, strengthen parent-school communications, increase student achievement, and encourage positive attitudes and good behavior.

It is hard to find time to meet, plan, and implement new practices, but there are ways to facilitate the work that must be done. Our principal helps us find time to meet and recognizes our contributions that improve the school. The School Action Team Chairperson distributes notes about the meetings to those who could not be present, and delegates extra tasks such as attending district-wide parent-advisory meetings or cluster meetings with other schools' Action Teams.

Before we formed SAT, "parental involvement" was viewed as the job of the parent liaison. But the task of informing and involving all families is too great for one person to handle. Many types of parental involvement were weak and ineffective. With a School Action Team (SAT), we have been able to focus on six types of involvement, across the grades, including activities at school and at home. Parents serve on the SIT and the SAT and are part of the decision-making process.

The results have been positive for our school. Good attitudes, mutual respect, meaningful relationships, and shared decision making continue to grow between school, home, and community.

School Stories

EXAMPLES OF THE SIX TYPES OF INVOLVEMENT

Type 6: Collaborating With the Community

Type 6 activities facilitate cooperation and collaboration among schools, families, and community groups, organizations, agencies, and individuals. The connections are two-way:

- Community resources help schools, families, and students.
- Educators, parents, and children help their communities.

Like families and schools, communities have significant roles to play in the education and well-being of youth. Within communities, there are many resources—human, economic, material, and social—that can support and enhance home and school activities. Type 6 activities identify and integrate these resources to improve schools, strengthen families, and assist students to succeed in school and in life.

Families and students need good information about the programs and services in their communities. Then, they can take advantage of enriching opportunities or obtain needed services.

Jackie Griswold, a master teacher in a Baltimore City elementary school, outlines some of the ways that her school collaborates with businesses, and other agencies and institutions in the local community. Her account illustrates how, despite limited school funds, a range of community connections can help schools and families help students accomplish important goals.

Sample Type 6 Activity

CONNECTING WITH OUR COMMUNITY

Reporter: Jackie Griswold, Master Teacher

Our school has a corporate partner that helps us organize many activities including recycling, tutoring, mentoring, and science-fair programs. When a problem arises, we canvas all of the businesses in the area for their help.

For example, when our playground was condemned, we wrote a grant with the help of the Community Association for new playground equipment. The grant required $15,000 in matching funds. Area businesses helped. Some small businesses, unable to provide funds, contributed in other ways. An area bowling alley provided the use of several alleys for one hour free of charge. Students got pledges from parents and relatives to pay a certain amount per pin they knocked down, and the money raised was donated to the school's playground fund. The student who raised the most money was awarded a pair of bowling shoes and a bowling ball donated by the bowling alley proprietor.

Our school offers students numerous activities in clubs sponsored by staff members, parents, and members of our community. These activities, a few of which are briefly described, provide students with positive opportunities to develop skills, talents, interests, and self-confidence.

An After-School Soccer Program uses a professional soccer pavilion near the school. Several teachers discussed their plans with the director of the pavilion and secured the use of the facilities free of charge. In addition, the director provided tee-shirts and trophies for the soccer players.

- A Say No To Drugs Club has been in operation for several years. Community service is stressed and partnerships have been formed with a community hospital and a nursing home. Students make pictures and holiday crafts to decorate the hospital. They also make gifts for the residents of the nursing home and sing for them at holiday time.

- An After-School Dance Club is free of charge to students through a partnership with an area recreation association.

- A Cheerleading Club is provided for the students with help from teachers, parents, and former students.

- After-School Karate and Gymnastics Clubs are led by parents who volunteered to offer these opportunities to students.

- An Art Club, Sewing Club, and Spanish Club are also offered to our students by staff and community members.

- We even found a club in the community to assist the school. Teachers visited a local senior citizens club and persuaded its members to come to read to first graders at the school once or twice a week. The first graders love their "Senior Readers" and look forward to seeing them.

The only financial costs to the school to develop connections with our community are to prepare and mail letters. The real investments are the time commitments by staff, parents, and community members. Our connections with the community have generated excitement about the new activities and the improved school climate. We will enthusiastically add activities involving community members and facilities to give students many positive experiences.

3

Conducting
Workshops

This chapter provides an outline and agenda for two workshops: Training and End-of-Year Celebration. The workshops may be conducted by state coordinators, district facilitators, or school leaders. Both workshops are designed for Action Teams for School, Family, and Community Partnerships or other audiences interested in developing programs of partnership. The workshops provide attendees with a common vocabulary, background, and processes that enable educators, parents, and others to talk and work together to build their programs of partnership.

The **Training Workshop** includes a warm-up activity, information on the six types of involvement, the Action Team approach, a focus on results, and next steps. It is outlined for a three-hour time period and for one day to give participants more opportunities to share ideas and information, take stock of their present practices and needs, and plan ahead. It may be expanded to two days to enable full Action Teams to complete their one-year action plans for improving partnerships.

The **End-of-Year Celebration Workshop** is conducted to recognize the progress that is made each year in improving school-family-community partnerships. It includes presentations on best practices, panel discussions on problems and solutions, school exhibits, and continuation plans. It is outlined for a full day but can be shortened to a half day.

The outlines, annotated guides, and workshop evaluations in this chapter may be used as directed, or adapted and improved to meet local needs and interests. Transparencies and handouts for the workshops can be made from the materials in Chapter 4. Forms from Chapters 5 and 6 of the handbook also are used in the workshops.

Training Workshops

SCHOOL-FAMILY-COMMUNITY CONNECTIONS: STRENGTHENING YOUR PROGRAM OF PARTNERSHIPS

Preplanning: Facilitators should review this handbook, paying attention to the workshop materials for presentations, discussions, and activities.

Time: At least three hours are needed to present the background information that Action Teams need to proceed with their work (see agenda for three-hour workshop).

The workshop may be lengthened to one full day (see agenda for one-day workshop). It may be expanded to two days *if* all the members of the Action Teams for School, Family, and Community Partnerships are in attendance, including the principal. The Action Teams should have knowledge of their schools' major goals and present partnership activities at all grade levels and should have collected some ideas from other teachers and parents about desired partnership activities.

Materials: Overhead projector, screen, chart paper for recording responses

Give attendees: An agenda
                    Paper copies of the transparencies that you use
                    Other useful handouts
                    A workshop evaluation

Overview: Facilitators should plan to balance their presentations of new information with opportunities for attendees to think and talk about the information and apply it to their own schools.

Whatever the length of the workshop, the goal is to help attendees on the following:

- Understand the framework of six types of involvement
- Recognize their starting points of present practices at their schools
- Understand the structure and members of an Action Team for School, Family, and Community Partnerships
- Understand that they must meet specific challenges to conduct a high-quality program
- Know that different practices of partnership lead to specific school goals and results
- Set a vision for the future using the Three-Year Outline
- Develop a One-Year Action Plan for the next school year

- In the short workshop (three hours), some basic information is shared and some applications conducted. In the one-day workshop, more information is presented, several applications and discussions are conducted, and some work on a long-term vision is initiated. On the second day of a two-day workshop, full Action Teams draft their One-Year Action Plans for later discussion at their schools.

- Ultimately, all Action Teams for School, Family, and Community Partnerships must write a One-Year Action Plan. Work not completed during a workshop is finished at the school site. Facilitators should obtain copies of each school's One-Year Action Plan to help each school develop its program of school-family-community partnerships.

Your Planning Notes: _____

_____

_____

_____

_____

_____

_____

_____

_____

_____

_____

_____

_____

_____

_____

_____

_____

_____

_____

_____

Sample Agendas for
Training Workshops

Training Workshops are conducted to provide members of Action Teams for School, Family, and Community Partnerships with the background they need in the six types of involvement and to help them get started in planning and implementing their programs.

Here are sample agendas that you can use or adapt for a *three-hour workshop* and for a *one-day workshop*. You may streamline the agendas to show only the titles of main topics and their time periods. Details are provided here for facilitators. The training workshops make use of the other materials in this handbook.

The three-hour workshop should include an overview and introduction to important topics. It might be scheduled in the morning—from 9 a.m. to noon, in the afternoon from noon to 3:00 p.m., in the evening from 3:30 p.m. to 6:30 p.m., or at other convenient times. You may choose to offer meals or snacks to the participants. Tables, chairs, microphones, folders, name tags, and other materials also will be needed for your workshop.

The one-day workshop should make good use of five to seven hours, including lunch. Breakfast and other snacks also may be provided. Door prizes or table centerpieces may be awarded at the end of the day. Stipends to the schools, planning grants, continuing education credits, and other recognitions may be awarded.

Transportation and child care for the parents on the Action Teams may be needed. As noted in the workshop outline, the one-day workshop can be expanded to two days (at the workshop site, or at the school site) to help Action Teams complete their One-Year Action Plans for their partnership programs.

The workshops are designed to prepare Action Teams for School, Family, and Community Partnerships to take leadership and work with others at their schools and in their communities. Facilitators also may offer workshops to other administrators, teachers, parents, and community members who will be involved in the work of the Action Teams.

Sample Agenda

SCHOOL-FAMILY-COMMUNITY CONNECTIONS: STRENGTHENING YOUR PROGRAM OF PARTNERSHIPS

9:00–9:10   **Welcome and Warm-up** (10 min.)

9:10–10:40   **The Six Types of Involvement and Action Team Approach**

Facilitator Overview: The six types of involvement and challenges (30 min.)

Group Activity: Starting Points—An Inventory of Present Practices (30 min.)

Facilitator: Structure of Action Team for School, Family, and Community Partnerships and Members of the Action Team (15 min.)

Group Activity: How to Organize an Action Team at Your School (15 min.)

10:40–10:50   **Break** (10 min.)

10:50–11:40   **Focus on Results**

Facilitator: Linking Six Types of Involvement to Specific Results (20 min.)

Group Activity: School Goals and Results of Partnerships (30 min.)

11:40–12:00   **Next Steps** (20 min.)

Descriptions of Three-Year Outlines and One-Year Action Plans
Facilitator's deadlines and assistance to Action Teams
Other topics (see one-day workshop agenda)
Questions and answers
Workshop evaluation

Sample Agenda

SCHOOL-FAMILY-COMMUNITY CONNECTIONS: STRENGTHENING YOUR PROGRAM OF PARTNERSHIPS

8:15–8:45	**Registration and Refreshments**
8:45–9:00	**Greetings and Introductions** (15 min.)
9:00–9:15	**Warm-up Activity** (15 min.)
9:15–10:15	**Facilitator:** Overview—The Six Types of Involvement (30 min.) **Group Activity:** Starting Points—An Inventory of Present Practices (30 min.)
10:15–10:30	**Break** (15 min.)
10:30–11:15	**Meeting the Challenges** **Facilitator:** Identifying the Challenges for the Six Types of Involvement (15 min.) **Group Activity:** Jumping Hurdles, and Report Out (30 min.)
11:15–12:00	**The Action Team Approach and Developing an Effective Action Team** (45 min.) **Facilitator:** Action Team Structure and Members of the Team (15 min.) **Group Activity:** Discuss How to Organize an Action Team at Your School (30 min.)
12:00–1:00	**Lunch** (provided *or* on own)
1:00–1:40	**Focus on Results** (40 min.) **Facilitator:** Linking the Six Types of Involvement to Specific Results (20 min.) **Group Activity:** School Goals and Results of Partnerships (20 min.)
1:40–2:40	**Looking Ahead—Three-Year Outlines** (1 hour) **Facilitator:** Planning Three-Year Sequences for Improving the Six Types of Involvement and Reaching School Goals (10 min.) **Group Activity:** Three-Year Outlines, and Report Out (50 min.)
2:40–3:00	**Next Steps** (20 min.) Descriptions of One-Year Action Plans Facilitator's deadlines and assistance to Action Teams Workshop evaluation, requirements for credits, parking, stipends, honoraria, awards, or other items to close the workshop

Note to Facilitators:

The topics in the above agenda give Action Teams the "basics" needed to plan and implement their programs of partnership. In your presentations, you may add examples of practices to meet the special needs of those attending your workshops. For example, if elementary, middle, and high school Action Teams attend, you should include in the overview and discussion of challenges some practices of partnership for different grade levels, or practices to ease transitions from one level of schooling to the next. If your schools have improvement teams or councils, you may want to discuss the work of these advisory or decision-making units and their links with Action Teams for School, Family, and Community Partnerships. You may add or substitute other topics in the workshop agendas to address specific needs or interests of your schools, families, and communities.

Components of Training Workshops

NOTES FOR FACILITATORS

I. WARM-UP ACTIVITY (10-15 minutes)

1. Distribute copies of **warm-up activity.** One example of a warm-up activity is "Are Two Heads Better Than One?" (provided for you at the end of this section). Give participants 2 minutes to work *alone* on this puzzle. Call "Time." Then ask the participants to work with one or more partners for 2 minutes to complete the activity. Ask participants to call out their answers for Items 1, 2, and so on.

2. Ask: **How did working together compare with working alone on this activity?** (List or just listen to the responses.) Possible replies: "Working as partners made the task easier." "We used each other's talents, strengths, and skills." "I didn't feel totally responsible for completing the task." "It was fun." (Many other responses are possible.)

3. Explain: **The same results occur when teachers, parents, students, and others work together to develop a comprehensive program of school, family, and community partnerships for their school. Today's workshop will help you see how to create and conduct an ongoing, positive program of partnerships. You will be offered ways to organize your work as an Action Team in order to implement activities, monitor progress, and continue to improve school-family-community connections over time.**

ALTERNATIVE WARM-UP ACTIVITY (10-15 minutes)

1. Ask attendees to pick a partner nearby. Assign: **Think of *one* successful activity that you have used or heard about to involve families at school or at home. You have 3 minutes each to share one example.** (Time this, and let participants know when it is the partner's turn to share an example.)

2. Call "Time." Ask: **Raise your hands if you heard a good idea that might be conducted *at school* to increase partnerships? at home? in the community? With large groups of parents? small groups? individually with one parent or family at time? in the early grades? older elementary? middle grades? high school? all grades?** (Attendees will raise their hands to indicate the many different ways that family involvement can occur.)

3. Explain: **The workshop today will help all of us understand the many different types of involvement that are needed in a comprehensive program of partnerships. We will better understand the practices that you are already conducting in your school, and will consider which practices you might want to add to your programs to help meet your school's specific goals. You will be offered ways to organize your work as an Action Team in order to implement activities, monitor progress, and continue to improve school-family-community connections over time.**

II. FRAMEWORK—SIX TYPES OF INVOLVEMENT

1. Introduce Epstein's six types of involvement. You may start by showing how school-family-community are "overlapping spheres of influence" (see diagrams for transparencies in Chapter 4).

2. Discuss the **Six Types of Involvement.** Use transparencies or paper copies of the transparencies to broadly describe each type. **If you have time,** you can add **sample practices** that support each type, **challenges** that need to be addressed, and **redefinitions** of traditional terms for involvement that are needed for today's families and schools. (It is a good idea to practice and time your presentation before the workshop.)

3. Ask for questions about the framework of six types of involvement.

    ■ Reinforce the idea that some practices are useful at all grade levels, but others will change as students move from grade to grade.

    ■ The challenges to reach all families must be met in order to have a successful program.

    ■ Students must be part of the partnership.

    ■ Progress is incremental. Improvements and additions are based on each school's starting point.

4. Show and describe the inventory called *Starting Points*. This checklist (in Chapter 5) should be included in the workshop packet and used immediately after the facilitator introduces the framework of six types of involvement. *Starting Points* allows workshop attendees to see that they are presently conducting many school-family-community connections for all or most of the six types of involvement. About 20 to 30 minutes are needed to complete *Starting Points*.

    ■ After presenting the framework of six types of involvement, let attendees know that they have already started building their program of partnerships with their *present practices*. Most schools, however, do not conduct all of the activities that are listed for each of the six types with families and students in different grade levels.

    ■ Ask attendees to fill in *Starting Points*. Only one person from each school team or workshop group needs to do the checking, but all should have copies of the inventory to discuss their present practices.

    ■ If time permits, ask a few volunteers to share what they learned about their schools' present practices by completing the inventory.

III. THE ACTION TEAM STRUCTURE

1. Show the Ten Steps to School-Family-Community Partnerships (transparency or handout in Chapter 4). Tell how these steps will be facilitated and supported to ensure each school's progress.

2. Show the diagram of the **Action Team Structure #1** (see chart in Chapter 4).

- Explain that the Action Team for Partnerships works as the "action arm" of the School Improvement Team (SIT) or other planning council. (If there is no planning group at a school, explain that the Action Team for Partnerships takes a lead role for improving school-family-community connections. If there is no SIT or council, discuss the committees for each type of involvement.)

- Show that the Action Team is linked to the SIT. It is suggested that one member of the Action Team also should be a member of the School Improvement Team or Council. The Action Team reports its plans and progress to the SIT on a regular schedule (e.g., twice a year).

- Show that each member of the Action Team for School, Family, and Community Partnerships serves as chair or co-chair of a committee for one of the six types of involvement. Additional teachers, parents, and others work with each committee chair to ensure that progress is made each year on all six types.

3. You also may show the **Action Team Structure #2** (see chart in Chapter 4.) Explain that this diagram shows an Action Team for *each* of the main goals for school improvement. For each of the school's goals, appropriate practices are selected and implemented from the six types of involvement to enable families and community members to help students and the school reach important goals. The members of the Action Team for Partnerships work with the other goal-oriented Action Teams and keep track of or recommend activities for school-family-community partnerships.

4. Show and discuss the chart **Members of the Action Team** (in Chapter 4). Explain the size of the team, members and their positions, terms of office, and leadership structure. Link your explanation back to the structure of the Action Team.

5. Ask for questions about the structure and members of the Action Team. **If there is time,** allow participants 10 to 15 minutes to discuss how their Action Team might link to their School Improvement Team and how it might conduct its work. Of course, these decisions cannot be made without consulting others at the school. They also could discuss how often the Action Team might meet, and how often it could report its work to the School Improvement Team, the full faculty, parents, students, parent organizations, and the community.

IV. MEETING THE CHALLENGES

Facilitators should include a discussion of the challenges that must be met to create an excellent program of partnerships.

1. Explain that most schools conduct some activities for each of the six types of involvement, but most have not met the challenges that make their programs inclusive of all families, at all grade levels, in ways that are clear, efficient, and family friendly. To develop high-quality programs, it is important to meet specific challenges for each of the six types of involvement. (Use examples from transparencies on CHALLENGES in Chapter 4.)

Note: In short three-hour workshops, the challenges should be discussed along with the overview of the six types of involvement, but there may not be enough time to use the transparencies on the challenges.

2. After a brief overview of the challenges and some examples of ways to meet them, ask the attendees to work together in school teams or workshop groups on this discussion activity:

   Jumping Hurdles (Question 2 from the Small Group Discussion Guide in Chapter 6). One person should record one or more school-family-community partnership activities that were successfully conducted at the school that required some challenge to be met or problem to be solved.

3. Allow at least 30 minutes for the groups to complete their discussions. Ask for at least three volunteers to share their reports with the large group.

V. FOCUS ON RESULTS

1. Discuss how various practices of school-family-community partnerships are linked to *different,* important results for students, families, and teachers. Explain that although many people think that any partnership activity will increase student achievement, that is NOT the case. Some activities do not directly affect student learning, but may produce other desired results. To develop high-quality programs and to write good program plans, it is important to know which results are expected from each of the six types of involvement. (Use examples from transparencies on RESULTS in Chapter 4.)

2. After a brief overview of some of the major results that may be expected from each type of involvement, ask the attendees to work together in school teams or workshop groups on this discussion activity:

   School Goals and Results of Partnerships (in Chapter 6). The group should identify *one* of the school's major and specific goals for students (e.g., attendance, achievement in reading, improved writing, better behavior). Then, one person should record the group's ideas of practices from the six types of involvement that should directly link to the stated goal. Explain that some goals may be assisted by one or two types of involvement, whereas other goals may be reached with practices from all six types of involvement.

3. Allow at least 30 minutes for the groups to complete their discussions. Ask for at least three volunteers to share their reports on one school goal and the practices of partnerships that link directly to that goal. The facilitator and audience should listen to see if they agree that the practices of partnership selected would directly contribute to the stated goal in the short term.

VI. LOOKING AHEAD: Three-Year Outline (Form A or Form B)

NOTE: Facilitators must choose Form A or Form B of the Three-Year Outline for the workshop attendees to use. Form A asks for long-term goals for each of the six types of involvement. Form B asks for a vision of how school-family-community partnerships might contribute to major school improvement goals set by a school (see Chapter 5 for these forms).

In a three-hour workshop, the facilitator shows and discusses the Three-Year Outline as one of the "next steps" that Action Teams will complete when they work together at their school site.

In a one-day workshop, the Three-Year Outline is the last activity of the day after attendees have completed *Starting Points* and the discussion activities.

1. **Explain that the Three-Year Outline is a brainstorming activity** that allows attendees to express their ideas on how practices of partnership might develop and improve over three years at their schools. Review the directions at the top of the form you select (Form A or Form B).

   Allocate at least one hour for teams to conduct this activity and share ideas. If members from the same school are attending, they should work together. If individuals are attending from different schools or from other administrative units, they should form work groups to share ideas and visions of future directions for partnerships in their schools. One person in each group should serve as a recorder.

2. **Sharing ideas on the Three-Year Outline (Report Out)**

   If you use Form A, ask for one volunteer to share the three steps the group designed to develop Type 1 activities over three years. The question is: What would you like to do in your school to improve Type 1-Parenting activities *next year, the year after,* and *the year after that* to assist parents in understanding their children and the school and to help the school understand its families? Then ask for other volunteers to share their ideas of how they might improve Types 2 through 6 over three years. The facilitator may offer feedback on whether the steps reported are feasible and whether the activities described are family friendly, inclusive, positive, and sensible for use in targeted grades or all grade levels.

   If you use Form B, ask for one volunteer to share one of the major goals their school has set, the results desired for that goal over the next three years, and how partnership activities for some or all of the six types of involvement might contribute to the desired results in Years 1, 2, and 3. The question is: How will school-family-community partnerships for each type of involvement help your school reach important goals over the *next three years*? Then ask for other volunteers to share one of their school goals, desired results, and how practices of partnership will help reach the desired results. The facilitator may offer feedback on whether the activities selected are really linked to the goals and desired results. Are the activities positive and feasible? Will they lead directly and in the short term to the specific goal?

   NOTE: The Three-Year Outline is an informal document for a school's own use. It may be discussed with a facilitator, School Improvement Team, faculty, parents, and students to gather ideas about the directions that all partners in education would like the school to take to better inform and involve all families in ways that help students succeed. It may become a formal document if the school wishes and may be updated informally every year to keep the Action Team's eye on future directions for the program.

VII. LOOKING AHEAD: One-Year Action Plan (Form A or Form B)

NOTE: Facilitators should choose Form A or Form B of the One-Year Action Plan to match Form A or Form B of the Three-Year Outline (in Chapter 5). Form A asks for a one-year plan that focuses on the development of the six types of involvement. Form B asks for a one-year plan that focuses on how the six types of involvement will contribute to specific school improvement goals.

Show and discuss the One-Year Action Plan (Form A or Form B). Explain that this is one of the "next steps" the Action Teams will complete by working together at their school sites.

In a two-day workshop, the second day is dedicated to completing the near-final One-Year Action Plan to be presented to other groups at the school for discussion, input, and approval.

The facilitator should emphasize to workshop attendees that the One-Year Action Plan asks for specifics about when activities will be conducted, the preparation needed, helpers, and results for each activity. It is important that the Action Team for School, Family, and Community Partnerships check that activities are scheduled from month to month in reasonable, feasible sequences and not all during one or two months. The Action Team also should check that the activities they plan are well designed and clearly focused on desired results for each type of involvement or for important school goals.

VIII. NEXT STEPS: After the Workshop

Ask participants to share with the whole group some of the next steps they will take to plan and implement a program of partnerships at their schools.

They may say that they need to review the ideas from the workshop with the principal (if he/she is not present), or with the School Improvement Team, the full faculty, the PTA/PTO, or other groups. They may say that they need to identify additional members of their Action Team including teachers, administrators, parents, and others so they can begin to formally organize their work.

NOTE: Facilitators should set a deadline for the Action Teams to complete and return their One-Year Action Plans. Also, let the Action Teams know how to contact you for assistance with their plans.

YOUR NOTES:

Other topics and information to tailor this workshop for your school(s):

_____

_____

_____

_____

_____

_____

Workshop Warm-Up

ARE TWO HEADS BETTER THAN ONE?

1. <u>**EGGS**</u>
   EASY

2. **PERSON   ALITY**

3. ma✔il

4. ɢʀoᴜ**ND**

5. timer timer

6. <u>**SLEEPING**</u>
       JOB

7.   house
   prairie

8.   c c
    garage
     r r

9. <u>**RISING**</u>
      IT

10.   c
      o
      m
      i
      c

11. 12safety345

12. **TAKE TAKE**

13. <u>**weather**</u>
    feeling

14. m ce
    m ce
    m ce

15.   s
      t
     one

16. **CA**ʙᴀɢ**T**

17.   **MOST**
          MOST
    FIRST **MOST**
          MOST

18. <u>**BACK**</u>
    TOP

19. I Right I

20. hair_____

Answers

ARE TWO HEADS BETTER THAN ONE?

1. eggs over easy

2. split personality

3. the check is in the mail

4. ground swell; gaining ground; higher ground

5. two-timer; double-timer

6. sleeping on the job

7. little house on the prairie

8. two-car garage

9. rising above it

10. stand-up comic; comic strip

11. safety in numbers; safety counts

12. double take; take two

13. feeling under the weather

14. three blind mice

15. cornerstone

16. cat's out of the bag

17. first and foremost

18. back on top

19. right between the eyes

20. receding hairline

Note: Audiences may think of other answers to the word puzzles.

Sample Agenda for
End-of-Year Celebration Workshop

Whether you are working with one school or many, it helps to have an end-of-year celebration and planning workshop to recognize the progress that was made and to plan ahead to improve partnerships during the next school year.

Here is a sample agenda for a one-day workshop in which participants share their best practices, discuss problems and solutions, and begin to update their Three-Year Outline and prepare their next One-Year Action Plan.

At the end-of-year celebration, each school is invited to display information on practices that they implemented to promote school-family-community partnerships. The exhibits may be set up on tables and include charts, photographs, slides, video- or audiotapes, handouts, or other communications. Schools are asked to label their activities according to the six types of involvement so that those who visit the displays will see how an activity might be used to strengthen particular parts of their program of partnerships. Attendees are given time to visit the exhibits and to talk with each other about their activities.

You may adapt this agenda (e.g., to two hours or a half day) if the Action Team members from only one school come together at the end of the year to report progress to the school faculty and all families. You may adapt the agenda and event in other ways to fit your schools and circumstances. For example, you might want to shorten or lengthen the time segments in the agenda depending on the work that has been accomplished, the number of problem-solving panels you wish to feature, the time needed at the workshop for small group discussions about future plans, and other topics.

If lunch is provided, the lunch break may be reduced to 40-45 minutes to provide more time for other agenda items. If attendees must go out for lunch, an hour is usually needed for travel to local restaurants. Tables and chairs for participants, microphones for presenters, and tables and other audiovisual equipment for exhibits also are needed.

Sample Agenda

———

SCHOOL-FAMILY-COMMUNITY PARTNERSHIPS:
CELEBRATING PROGRESS AND PLANNING AHEAD

8:30–9:00	**Registration and Refreshments**
9:00–9:30	**Greetings and Introductions**
9:30–10:30	**Action Team Presentations of Best Practices**
10:30–10:45	**Break**
10:45–11:15	**Continuation—Action Team Presentations of Best Practices**
11:15–Noon	**Gathering Ideas—Visits to School Exhibits**
Noon–1:00	**Lunch** (provided *or on own*)
1:00–2:00	**Meeting the Challenges—Panel Presentations**
2:00–3:00	**Next Steps—Continuation Plans** **Updating One-Year Action Plans and** **Three-Year Outlines**
3:00–3:30	**Wrap Up / Report Out / Final Announcements**
	Workshop Evaluation

Sample Agenda

WITH NOTES FOR FACILITATORS

8:30–9:00   **Registration and Refreshments**

9:00–9:30   **Greetings and Introductions**

Overview and goals for the day

9:30–11:15   **Action Team Presentations on Best Practices**

(See information on planning needed for this time segment later in this chapter.)

     9:30–10:00   **Schools Selected to Present Best Practices on Type 1 (Parenting) and Type 2 (Communicating)**

This might include presentations on a particularly effective parenting program that gets information to those who cannot come; an unusually effective newsletter that includes two-way communications from home to school and school to home; an unusual conference schedule in high schools; or other successful Type 1 and Type 2 activities that meet important challenges, such as including all families, etc.

     10:00–10:30   **Schools Selected to Present Best Practices on Type 3 (Volunteering) and Type 4 (Learning at Home)**

This might include presentations on a particularly successful way to engage volunteers at school and at home; a way for students to share what they are learning in math, science, English, or other subjects with their families; or other successful Type 3 and Type 4 activities that meet important challenges.

     10:30–10:45   **Break**

     10:45–11:15   **Schools Selected to Present Best Practices on Type 5 (Decision Making) and Type 6 (Collaborating With the Community)**

This might include presentations on particularly effective practices that parent leaders use to gather and give information to the families they represent; unusual community partnerships that reach families and students; or other successful Type 5 and Type 6 activities that meet important challenges.

11:15–Noon   **Gathering Ideas from School Exhibits on the Six Types of Involvement**

Facilitators may meet with Action Teams before the end-of-year celebration to discuss the most effective practices and modes of presentation for the school displays. Action Teams may wish to prepare short and clear summaries of some practices that would help other schools adopt or adapt the practices. Summaries should include names and phone numbers to call with any questions.

Sample Agenda

_____

continued

Noon–1:00	**Lunch** (provided *or* on own)

1:00–2:00   **Meeting the Challenges—Panel Presentations**

(See information on planning needed for this time segment later in this chapter.)

2:00–3:00   **Next Steps—Continuation Plans**
Updating Three-Year Outlines and One-Year Action Plans

Each school's Action Team meets to consider the various issues discussed in the morning, at the exhibits, and by the panels. Each Action Team should bring and refer to its own School Improvement Plan. The goal is to discuss how to update the Three-Year Outline and to consider what might be given priority on the One-Year Action Plan for the next school year. These discussions, decisions, and plans may be reviewed, discussed, and started at the workshop, but will be completed at the school site before the end of the school year. One-Year Action Plans include the work that will be conducted during the summer to prepare for the start of the next school year.

Each Action Team should select a reporter to share in the Wrap Up session one or two major new directions the school will take in the next year.

3:00–3:30   **Wrap Up**

Action Team Updates: Each Action Team reports one or two major plans discussed for their Three-Year Outline and One-Year Action Plan. (Note: This may be incorporated in the prior time segment if there are many final announcements.)

Final Announcements: The content of the final time period must be tailored for each workshop. Facilitators might include deadlines for updated plans; how to contact the facilitator for assistance; requirements for professional credit for attending the workshop (if appropriate); workshop evaluation; honoraria (if appropriate); awards (if planned ahead for unusual progress and excellence); door prizes (if planned); and other information for the schools.

End-of-Year Celebration Workshop

NOTES FOR FACILITATORS

The agenda for the End-of-Year Celebration Workshop includes two segments that require *advanced planning* by the workshop facilitator and participants: the presentations by participants of *best practices* and presentations by panelists on *meeting the challenges* for successful programs of partnership.

ADVANCED PLANNING is needed for this segment of the agenda:
9:30–11:15 Action Team Presentations on Best Practices

As they meet with the Action Teams throughout the year, facilitators should identify especially promising practices at the various schools and grade levels. Presenters should be selected to represent different schools and different grade levels to share outstanding activities at the end-of-year celebration.

Presenters should be notified ahead of time, informed of the time limits for their presentations in each segment, and guided in good presentation skills. The Action Team's chairperson may represent the school in these presentations or another effective speaker or group of speakers may be selected. They may use visual displays such as overheads, slides, charts, banners, or handouts. The print or pictures must be large enough for all to see.

It should be made clear to all workshop participants that a few activities were selected for presentation during this time period of the workshop, but many other good practices also are featured in the school exhibits.

The time from 9:30 to 11:15 a.m. can be planned in 15-minute segments for presentations on best practices for each of the six types of involvement, with a 15-minute break in the middle. For example, presenters for Types 1 and 2 share the time from 9:30 to 10 a.m. If *one* presenter is selected to describe one Type 1 and one Type 2 activity, each will have about 10 minutes for the presentation and 5 minutes for questions from the audience. If three presenters are selected for each type of involvement, each will have about 3 minutes for the presentation and a few minutes at the end for questions from the audience. Facilitators must decide how to use the time and select presenters accordingly.

An alternative use of time may be selected if schools meet in "clusters" during the school year. Under this plan, the 9:30-11:15 a.m. time segment for sharing best practices would be divided to give the clusters of schools equal time for their presentations on best practices. Facilitators should meet with Action Team chairpersons to decide which practices they present at the workshop. Across clusters, all six types of involvement should be represented.

It is the facilitator's responsibility at the workshop to keep presenters *on time*. This can best be accomplished by planning for these presentations prior to the workshop. It sometimes is necessary to signal presenters when they have one minute left to conclude their presentation.

**ADVANCED PLANNING is needed for this segment of the agenda
1:00–2:00 Meeting the Challenges — Panel Presentations**

Facilitators should identify especially important topics that have posed challenges to the Action Teams throughout the year. Usually, schools struggle with similar or related problems, and some schools solve them sooner than others and in varied ways. It should be made clear that the topics selected for the workshop are not the only important issues for discussion, but they do highlight a few challenges that may be particularly helpful to discuss.

The topics selected may address (a) the "challenges" linked to each type of involvement (in Chapter 4); (b) the organization and work of the Action Team; (c) linking and reporting to the School Improvement Team; (d) linking partnerships to school improvement goals; (e) forms of support from principals for the work of Action Teams (a panel of principals); (f) measuring results of specific practices; and (g) other important issues.

Panel participants should be selected to represent various views or different solutions and may include teachers, parents, students, principals, district leaders, or others from varied grade or school levels. Panel members should be selected for particular topics prior to the workshop, informed of the time allotted, and guided in effective presentation skills.

Three to five panels may be scheduled in one hour, with three to five participants on each panel sharing their experiences and observations. Time should be allotted for questions from the audience. For example, speakers would have about *3 minutes* for their summaries if there were three panels each with five people from different schools, or five panels each with three people from different schools. About 15 minutes would remain for questions from the audience. A smaller number of topics or participants would give more time for presentations and for questions.

At a recent workshop, one panel of eight people (four from each of two schools) focused on how they organized the work and meetings of their Action Teams in different ways. They addressed four questions to help other schools that were still struggling to create an effective team structure: Who is on your Action Team? When do you find time to meet? How do you keep in touch with your School Improvement Team, faculty, and families? What budget or fund-raising is needed to support the work of your Action Team? Half an hour was allocated at the workshop for this panel's presentation. Two people (one from each school) addressed each of the four questions with a 3-minute summary. This left about 6 minutes for questions from the audience. In the second half hour for panel presentations, a second panel of four people (two from each of the two different schools) addressed the topic of how to measure results of particular practices of partnership. Thus, in one hour, two panels addressed topics that were of interest to just about all schools attending the workshop.

Topics to consider for panel presentations:

- Budgets and fund-raising for school-family-community partnership activities
- Organizing productive "cluster" meetings of several schools during the school year
- Evaluating whether particular practices are effective, and for whom
- How a school improvement team or school council works effectively

- Identifying and connecting with "hard-to-reach" families—invited panel of parents, other family members, and educators
- Understanding each of the types of involvement at different grade levels
- Understanding the views and wishes of families—invited panel of diverse parents
- Understanding students' views of the help they need from school, family, and community to succeed in school—invited panel of students
- Meeting specific challenges for each type of involvement
- Specific topics of importance in your school and community

Evaluation
———

WORKSHOP ON SCHOOL-FAMILY-COMMUNITY PARTNERSHIPS

Date_____

Please circle how much you agree or disagree with each statement.

	Strongly Disagree	Disagree	Agree	Strongly Agree
Structure				
The goals of this workshop were clear.	SD	D	A	SA
The goals of this workshop were met.	SD	D	A	SA
Time was used well.	SD	D	A	SA
Content				
I gained many ideas that will help me or my school.	SD	D	A	SA
I feel better prepared to use or improve school, family, and community partnerships.	SD	D	A	SA
There were opportunities to share ideas with others.	SD	D	A	SA
Overall, this workshop was worthwhile.	SD	D	A	SA
Facilities				
The room was suitable.	SD	D	A	SA
Refreshments were satisfactory.	SD	D	A	SA

Other comments or ideas on the workshop:

_____

_____

_____

What assistance or follow-up would you like?

_____

_____

_____

Thank you for your reactions!

Evaluation

WORKSHOP ON SCHOOL-FAMILY-COMMUNITY PARTNERSHIPS

Date_____

How helpful were these workshop topics?

Check (✔) how helpful these were to you.

	Very Helpful	Helpful	Not Helpful
Background			
1. Understanding the six types of involvement and examples of practices	_____	_____	_____
2. Understanding and improving the work of School Improvement Teams	_____	_____	_____
3. Linking the work of your Action Team for School, Family, and Community Partnerships to your school goals and desired results	_____	_____	_____
Team Discussions			
1. Taking stock of your present practices—strengths, weaknesses, hard-to-reach families	_____	_____	_____
2. Gathering ideas for your school's plans for strengthening all six types of involvement in your program of partnerships	_____	_____	_____

Other comments or ideas on the workshop:

_____

_____

_____

What assistance or follow-up would you like?

_____

_____

_____

Thank you for your reactions!

4

Materials for Presentations and Workshops

This chapter provides charts, diagrams, and summaries that you may use as transparencies on overhead projectors or as printed handouts in your presentations and discussions with teachers, parents, and others. For the technologically inclined, these pages can be scanned for a computer file, made into color transparencies, or activated for computerized presentations. If you wish, you may revise the wording to match vocabulary used in your school, district, or state. Background information and references for these charts are in Chapter 1 of this handbook.

Included in this chapter are charts for the following:

Theoretical Model of Overlapping Spheres of Influence

1. **External Structure.** This shows the three contexts that influence children's learning and development. The areas of "overlap" indicate that the family, school, and community share responsibility for children. Various practices, philosophies, histories, and other forces create more or less overlap—more or fewer connections of the three contexts. The practices and extent of overlap change over time.

2. **Internal Structure.** This shows the interactions that may be activated when people in schools, families, and communities communicate and work together. The *child* is the central focus of and actor in these interactions. The connections of home, school, and community may be at an *institutional* level, involving all families, children, educators, and the community, or at the *individual* level, involving one teacher, parent, child, community partner, or small group.

Keys to Successful Partnerships

This is a one-page summary of the six types of involvement.

Summaries of the Six Types of School, Family, and Community Partnerships

Set A: **The Six Types of Involvement.** This set outlines a few of the *topics* that define each type of involvement.

Set B: **Sample *Practices* for Each Type.** This set shows a few examples of common practices for each type of involvement that have been effectively implemented in many elementary, middle, and high schools.

Set C: **Sample *Challenges* and *Redefinitions* for Each Type.** This set shows a few examples of program-design features that schools must address in order to have a truly successful program of partnerships.

Set D: **Sample *Results* From Each Type for Students, Parents, and Teachers.** This set shows a few examples of benefits that have been measured or observed for each type of involvement. The lists alert participants to the fact that *different results* are linked to *each type* of involvement. Practices should be selected or designed to maximize chances of reaching specific goals set by each school.

Note: Set A is the basic set for use in training workshops. Sets B, C, and D may be used in extended workshops, in follow-up meetings and discussions, or as printed handouts for Action Teams for School, Family, and Community Partnerships to use for planning purposes.

The four sets of summaries are drawn from the tables in Chapter 1 of this handbook. You may use them to give your audience an overview of the six types of involvement (Set A), and to encourage participants to raise questions or think of other examples of practices, challenges, needed redefinitions, and results that they have observed or measured (Sets B, C, and D). The summaries should help Action Teams understand and select practices for their partnership programs.

Ten Steps Toward Partnerships

This page lists the steps that must be taken to develop a strong and permanent program of school, family, and community partnerships.

Action Team Structure

These pages illustrate two ways to organize the work of an Action Team for School, Family, and Community Partnerships. Both charts assume that there is a school improvement team or school council to which the Action Team reports. If there is no such policy-setting body that sets goals and priorities for the school, remove the top box from these charts.

Members of the Action Team

This chart shows who should serve on an Action Team. There is flexibility in the number of members, their positions, terms of office, and leadership roles to ensure the formation of an effective Action Team that will work best in each school.

The ABCs of Action Team Leadership

These pages outline the qualities and responsibilities of the chair or co-chairs of the Action Team. They include guidelines to *A*ccount for team members, *B*e ready to share leadership, *C*ommunicate with all partners, *D*evelop good plans, *E*nsure progress, and *F*oster team spirit. It is important for the leaders of an Action Team to have these skills in order to help all team members work well together and accomplish their plans for partnership.

Levels of Commitment to Partnerships

Two pages list and explain the *levels* of commitment to partnerships. All six types of involvement are important. They are "types," not "levels." They lead to different, important results for students, families, and schools. There are, however, *levels of commitment* that increase this caring to civility, clarity, cooperation, and collaboration. A comprehensive program of partnerships will include all six types of involvement and work toward the highest level of commitment—collaboration.

Questions to Ask

This set of questions focuses attention on examples of basic practices for the six types of involvement. The series "Do You Have . . . ?" may be used to encourage Action Teams and workshop attendees to discuss some basic issues about comprehensive programs of partnership.

District and State Leadership Roles

Two charts summarize *some* of the activities that districts and states may choose to demonstrate their leadership, support, and encouragement for school, family, and community partnerships.

District leaders should (a) establish district policies and procedures that facilitate the work of the Action Teams in all schools and (b) identify and coordinate all district-level programs and activities with families and communities.

State leaders should (a) establish state policies and procedures that help all districts help all schools develop strong programs of partnership and (b) identify and coordinate all state-level programs and activities with families and communities.

Theoretical Model
OVERLAPPING SPHERES OF INFLUENCE OF FAMILY, SCHOOL, AND COMMUNITY ON CHILDREN'S LEARNING
External Structure

Force A
Time/Age/Grade Level

Force B
Experience, Philosophy, Practices of Family

Force C
Experience, Philosophy, Practices of School

Force D
Experience, Philosophy, Practices of Community

FAMILY

SCHOOL

COMMUNITY

Theoretical Model
OVERLAPPING SPHERES OF INFLUENCE*
Internal Structure

FAMILY　　　SCHOOL

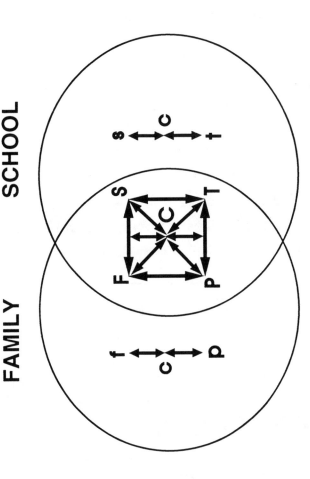

KEY:

Intra-institutional interactions (non-overlapping areas)
Inter-institutional interactions (overlapping area)

f/F = Family　c/C = Child　s/S = School　p/P = Parent　t/T = Teacher

Interactions include those at the institutional level (e.g., all families, children, educators, and entire community) and at the individual level (e.g., one parent, child, teacher, community partner).

In the full model the internal structure is extended to include the community: co/CO = Community　a/A = Agent from Community/Business

*Note:

THE KEYS TO SUCCESSFUL
SCHOOL-FAMILY-COMMUNITY PARTNERSHIPS
EPSTEIN'S SIX TYPES OF INVOLVEMENT

PARENTING: Assist families with parenting and child-rearing skills, understanding child and adolescent development, and setting home conditions that support children as students at each age and grade level. Assist schools in understanding families.

COMMUNICATING: Communicate with families about school programs and student progress through effective school-to-home and home-to-school communications.

VOLUNTEERING: Improve recruitment, training, work, and schedules to involve families as volunteers and audiences at the school or in other locations to support students and school programs.

LEARNING AT HOME: Involve families with their children in learning activities at home, including homework and other curriculum-related activities and decisions.

DECISION MAKING: Include families as participants in school decisions, governance, and advocacy through PTA/PTO, school councils, committees, and other parent organizations.

COLLABORATING WITH THE COMMUNITY: Coordinate resources and services for families, students, and the school with businesses, agencies, and other groups, and provide services to the community.

Epstein's Six Types of Involvement

1. **PARENTING:**
   BASIC RESPONSIBILITIES OF FAMILIES

2. **COMMUNICATING:**
   BASIC RESPONSIBILITIES OF SCHOOLS

3. **VOLUNTEERING:**
   INVOLVEMENT AT and
   FOR THE SCHOOL

4. **LEARNING AT HOME:**
   INVOLVEMENT IN
   ACADEMIC ACTIVITIES

5. **DECISION MAKING:**
   PARTICIPATION AND LEADERSHIP

6. **COLLABORATING WITH THE**
   COMMUNITY: COORDINATION OF
   RESOURCES AND SERVICES

Type 1

PARENTING

Basic Responsibilities of Families

✔ **Housing, health, nutrition, clothing, safety**

✔ **Parenting skills for all age levels**

✔ **Home conditions that support children as students at all grade levels**

✔ **Information and activities to help schools understand children and families**

Type 2

COMMUNICATING

Basic Responsibilities of Schools

SCHOOL-TO-HOME

✔ **Memos, notices, report cards, conferences, newsletters, phone calls, computerized messages**

✔ **Information to help families**
- **understand school programs and children's progress**
- **understand student tests and assessments**
- **choose or change schools**
- **choose or change courses, placements, programs, and activities**

HOME-TO-SCHOOL

✔ **2-Way channels of communication for questions and interactions**

Type 3

VOLUNTEERING

Involvement At and For the School

VOLUNTEERS

In School or Classroom

✔ **Assist administrators, teachers, students, or parents as mentors, coaches, boosters, monitors, lecturers, chaperones, tutors, leaders, demonstrators, and in other ways**

For School or Classroom

✔ **Assist school programs and children's progress from any location at any time**

AUDIENCES

✔ **Attend assemblies, performances, sports events, recognition and award ceremonies, celebrations, and other events**

Type 4

LEARNING AT HOME

Involvement in Academic Activities

INFORMATION FOR FAMILIES ON

✔ **How to help at home with homework**

✔ **Required skills to pass each subject**

✔ **Curriculum-related decisions**

✔ **Other skills and talents**

Type 5

DECISION MAKING

Participation and Leadership

✔ **PTA/PTO**
  - **membership, participation, leadership, representation**

✔ **Advisory councils**
  - **school improvement teams**
  - **Title I councils**
  - **school-site management**

✔ **Committees**

✔ **Independent school advisory groups**

School, Family, and Community Partnerships by J. L. Epstein et al., © 1997 Corwin Press, Inc.

Type 6

COLLABORATING
WITH THE COMMUNITY

✔ **Connections to enable the community to contribute to schools, students, and families**

- **Business partners**

- **Agencies**

- **Cultural groups**

- **Health services**

- **Recreation**

- **Other groups and programs**

✔ **Connections to enable schools, students and families to contribute to the community**

Sample Practices—Type I

PARENTING

Assist Families with Parenting Skills and Setting Home Conditions to Support Children as Students, and Assist Schools to Understand Families

✔ **Workshops, videotapes, computerized phone messages on parenting and child development at each age and grade level**

✔ **Parent education and other courses or training for parents (e.g., GED, family literacy, college or training programs)**

✔ **Family support programs to assist families with health, nutrition, and parenting, including clothing swap shops, food co-ops, parent-to-parent groups**

✔ **Home visiting programs or neighborhood meetings to help families understand schools and to help schools understand families**

✔ **Annual survey for families to share information and concerns with schools about their children's goals, strengths, and special talents**

Sample Practices—Type 2

COMMUNICATING

Conduct Effective Communications From School to Home and From Home to School About School Programs and Children's Progress

✔ **Conferences with every parent at least once a year with follow-ups as needed**

✔ **Language translators to assist families as needed**

✔ **Folders of student work sent home weekly or monthly for parent review and comments**

✔ **Parent and student pickup of report cards**

✔ **Regular schedule of useful notices, memos, phone calls, and other communications**

✔ **Effective newsletters including information about school events, student activities, and parents' questions, reactions, and suggestions**

✔ **Clear information about choosing schools, and selecting courses, programs, and activities within schools**

✔ **Clear information on all school policies, programs, reforms, assessments, and transitions**

✔ **Annual survey of families on students' needs and families' reactions to school programs**

Sample Practices—Type 3

VOLUNTEERING

Organize Volunteers and Audiences to Support the School and Students

✔ Annual survey to identify interests, talents, and availability of volunteers

✔ Parent room or family center for volunteer work, meetings, and resources for families

✔ Class parents, telephone tree, or other structures to provide all families with needed information

✔ Parent patrols to increase school safety

✔ Annual review of schedules for students' performances, sports events, and assemblies for daytime and evening audiences

Sample Practices—Type 4

LEARNING AT HOME

Involve Families With Their Children on Homework and Other Curriculum-Related Activities and Decisions

✔ **Information for families on required skills in all subjects at each grade**

✔ **Information on homework policies and how to monitor and discuss schoolwork at home**

✔ **Information on how to assist students with skills that they need to improve**

✔ **Regular schedule of homework that requires students to demonstrate and discuss what they are learning in class**

✔ **Calendars with daily or weekly activities for parents and students to do at home or in the community**

✔ **Summer learning packets or activities**

✔ **Family participation in helping students set academic goals each year and plan for college or work**

Sample Practices—Type 5

DECISION MAKING

Include Families as Participants in School Decisions, and Develop Parent Leaders and Representatives

✔ Active **PTA/PTO** or other parent organizations, advisory councils, or committees (e.g., curriculum, safety, personnel) for parent leadership and participation

✔ **Action Team for School, Family, and Community Partnerships** to oversee the development of the school's program with practices for all six types of involvement

✔ District-level advisory councils and committees

✔ Information on school or local elections for school representatives

✔ Networks to link all families with parent representatives

✔ Independent advocacy groups to lobby for school reform and improvements

Sample Practices—Type 6

COLLABORATING WITH THE COMMUNITY

Coordinate Resources and Services From the Community for Families, Students, and the School, and Provide Services to the Community

✔ **Information for students and families on community health, cultural, recreational, social support, and other programs or services**

✔ **Information on community activities that link to learning skills and talents, including summer programs for students**

✔ **"One-stop" shopping for family services through partnerships of school, counseling, health, recreation, job training, and other agencies**

✔ **Service to the community by students, families, and schools (e.g., art, music, drama, and activities for senior citizens; recycling projects; tutoring or coaching programs; and others)**

✔ **Participation of alumni in school programs for students**

✔ **School-business partnerships**

Challenges—Type 1

PARENTING

✔ **Provide information to *all* families who want it or who need it, not just to the few who attend workshops or meetings at the school building**

✔ **Enable families to share information with schools about background, culture, children's talents, goals, and needs**

✔ **Make all information for families clear, usable, age-appropriate, and linked to children's success**

Redefinitions

"Workshop" is not only a *meeting* on a topic held at the school building at a particular time but also the *content* of a topic to be viewed, heard, or read at convenient times and varied locations.

Challenges—Type 2
COMMUNICATING

✔ **Make all memos, notices, and other print and non-print communications clear and understandable for all families**

✔ **Consider parents who do not speak English well, do not read well, or need large type**

✔ **Obtain ideas from families to improve the design and content of major communications such as newsletters, report cards, and conference schedules**

✔ **Establish an easy-to-use two-way channel for communications from school to home and from home to school**

Redefinitions

"Communications about school programs and student progress" are not only from school to home but also include two-way, three-way, and many-way channels of communication that connect schools, families, students, and the community.

Challenges—Type 3

VOLUNTEERING

✔ **Recruit widely for volunteers so that *all* families know that their time and talents are welcome**

✔ **Make flexible schedules for volunteers, assemblies, and events to enable working parents to participate**

✔ **Provide training for volunteers, and match time and talent with school needs**

Redefinitions

"Volunteer" not only means those who come to school during the day, but also those who support school goals and children's learning in any way, at any place, and at any time.

Challenges—Type 4

LEARNING AT HOME

✔ **Design and implement a regular schedule of interactive homework (e.g., weekly or twice a month) for which students take responsibility to discuss important things they are learning with their families**

✔ **Coordinate family-linked interactive homework assignments if students have several teachers**

✔ **Involve families and their children in all important curriculum-related decisions**

Redefinitions

"Homework" not only means work that students do alone, but also interactive activities that students share with others at home or in the community, linking schoolwork to real life.

"Help" at home means how families encourage, listen, react, praise, guide, monitor, and discuss schoolwork with their children, not how they "teach" children school subjects.

Challenges—Type 5

DECISION MAKING

✔ **Include parent leaders from all racial, ethnic, socioeconomic, and other groups in the school**

✔ **Offer training to enable parent leaders to develop skills to serve as representatives of other families**

✔ **Include student representatives along with parents in decision-making**

Redefinitions

"Decision making" means a process of partnership, of shared views and actions toward shared goals, not just a power struggle between conflicting ideas.

Parent "leader" means a representative who shares information with and obtains ideas from other families and community members, not just a parent who attends school meetings.

Challenges—Type 6

COLLABORATING WITH THE COMMUNITY

✔ **Solve turf problems of roles, responsibilities, funds, and places for collaborative activities**

✔ **Inform all families and students about community programs and services**

✔ **Assure equal opportunities for students and families to obtain services or participate in community programs**

✔ **Match business and community volunteers and resources with school goals**

Redefinitions

"**Community" means not only the neighborhoods where students' homes and schools are located, but also all neighborhoods or locations that influence their learning and development.**

"**Community" is rated not only by low or high social or economic qualities, but also by strengths and talents available to support students, families, and schools.**

"**Community" includes not only families with children in the schools, but also all who are interested in and affected by the quality of education.**

Results—Type I

PARENTING*

RESULTS FOR STUDENTS

- **Awareness of family supervision**
- **Respect for parents**
- **Positive personal qualities, habits, beliefs, and values taught by family**
- **Balance between time spent on chores, other activities, and homework**
- **Regular attendance**
- **Awareness of importance of school**

RESULTS FOR PARENTS

- **Self-confidence about parenting**
- **Knowledge of child and adolescent development**
- **Adjustments in home environment as children proceed through school**
- **Awareness of own and others' challenges in parenting**
- **Feeling of support from school and other parents**

RESULTS FOR TEACHERS

- **Understanding of families' backgrounds, cultures, concerns, goals, needs, and views of their children**
- **Respect for families' strengths and efforts**
- **Understanding of student diversity**
- **Awareness of own skills to share information on child development**

*This chart refers to results of well-designed and well-implemented Type I practices.

School, Family, and Community Partnerships by J. L. Epstein et al., © 1997 Corwin Press, Inc.

Results—Type 2

COMMUNICATING*

RESULTS FOR STUDENTS

- Awareness of own progress in subjects and skills
- Knowledge of actions needed to maintain or improve grades
- Understanding of school programs and policies
- Informed decisions about courses and programs
- Awareness of own role as courier and communicator in school-family partnerships

RESULTS FOR PARENTS

- Understanding of school programs and policies
- Monitoring and awareness of child's progress in subjects and skills
- Responses to student problems
- Ease of interactions and communications with school and teachers
- High rating of school quality

RESULTS FOR TEACHERS

- Diversity of communications with families
- Ability to communicate clearly
- Use of network of parents to communicate with all families
- Ability to understand family views and elicit help with children's progress

*This chart refers to results of well-designed and well-implemented Type 2 practices.

School, Family, and Community Partnerships by J. L. Epstein et al., © 1997 Corwin Press, Inc.
Photocopying permissible for local school use only.

Results—Type 3
VOLUNTEERING*

RESULTS FOR STUDENTS

- Skills in communicating with adults
- Skills that are tutored or taught by volunteers
- Awareness of many skills, talents, occupations, and contributions of parents and other volunteers

RESULTS FOR PARENTS

- Understanding of the teacher's job
- Self-confidence about ability to work in school and with children
- Awareness that families are welcome and valued at school
- Specific skills of volunteer work
- Use of school activities at home
- Enrollment in programs to improve own education

RESULTS FOR TEACHERS

- Organization, training, and use of volunteers
- Readiness to involve families in new ways, including those who do not volunteer at school
- Awareness of parents' talents and interests in school and children
- Individual attention to students because of help from volunteers

*This chart refers to results of well-designed and well-implemented Type 3 practices.

Results—Type 4

LEARNING AT HOME*

RESULTS FOR STUDENTS

- Skills, abilities, and test scores linked to homework and classwork
- Homework completion
- Positive attitude about homework and school
- View of parent as more similar to teacher and of home as more similar to school
- Self-confidence in ability as learner

RESULTS FOR PARENTS

- Knowledge of how to support, encourage, and help student at home each year
- Discussions of school, classwork, homework, and future plans
- Understanding of instructional program and what child is learning in each subject
- Appreciation of teacher's skills
- Awareness of child as a learner

RESULTS FOR TEACHERS

- Varied designs of homework including interactive assignments
- Respect of family time
- Recognition of helpfulness of single-parent, dual-income, and all families in motivating and reinforcing student learning
- Satisfaction with family involvement and support

*This chart refers to results of well-designed and well-implemented Type 4 practices.

Results—Type 5

DECISION MAKING*

RESULTS FOR STUDENTS

- Awareness of representation of families in school decisions
- Understanding that student rights are protected
- Specific benefits linked to policies enacted by parent organizations

RESULTS FOR PARENTS

- Input into policies that affect children's education
- Feeling of ownership of school
- Awareness of parents' voices in school decisions
- Shared experiences and connections with other families
- Awareness of school, district, and state policies

RESULTS FOR TEACHERS

- Awareness of perspectives of families in policy development and school decisions
- Acceptance of equality of family representatives of school committees and in leadership roles

*This chart refers to results of well-designed and well-implemented Type 5 practices.

Results—Type 6

COLLABORATING WITH THE COMMUNITY*

RESULTS FOR STUDENTS

- Skills and talents from enriched curricular and extracurricular experiences
- Knowledge and exploration of careers and options for future education and work
- Self-confidence, feeling valued by and belonging to the community
- Positive relationships with adults in the community

RESULTS FOR PARENTS

- Knowledge and use of local resources to increase skills and talents or to obtain needed services
- Interactions with other families in community activities
- Awareness of community's contributions to the school
- Participation in activities to strengthen the community

RESULTS FOR TEACHERS

- Knowledge and use of community resources to enrich curriculum and instruction
- Skill in working with mentors, business partners, community volunteers, and others to assist students and teaching practice
- Knowledge of referral processes for families and children with needs for specific services

*This chart refers to results of well-designed and well-implemented Type 6 practices.

Ten Steps to
School-Family-Community Partnerships

✔ **Create an Action Team for Partnerships**

✔ **Obtain funds and official support**

✔ **Provide training and guidelines to Action Team members**

✔ **Identify starting points—present strengths and weaknesses**

✔ **Develop a three-year outline**

✔ **Write a one-year action plan**

✔ **Enlist staff, parents, students, and community members to help conduct activities**

✔ **Evaluate implementations and results**

✔ **Conduct annual celebrations and report progress to all participants**

✔ **Continue working toward a comprehensive, on-going, positive program of partnerships**

Action Team Structure #1

SCHOOL IMPROVEMENT TEAM

ACTION TEAM for SCHOOL, FAMILY, and COMMUNITY PARTNERSHIPS

Committee for TYPE 1 Parenting	Committee for TYPE 2 Communicating	Committee for TYPE 3 Volunteering	Committee for TYPE 4 Learning at Home	Committee for TYPE 5 Decision Making	Committee for TYPE 6 Collaborating with Community

Action Team Structure #2

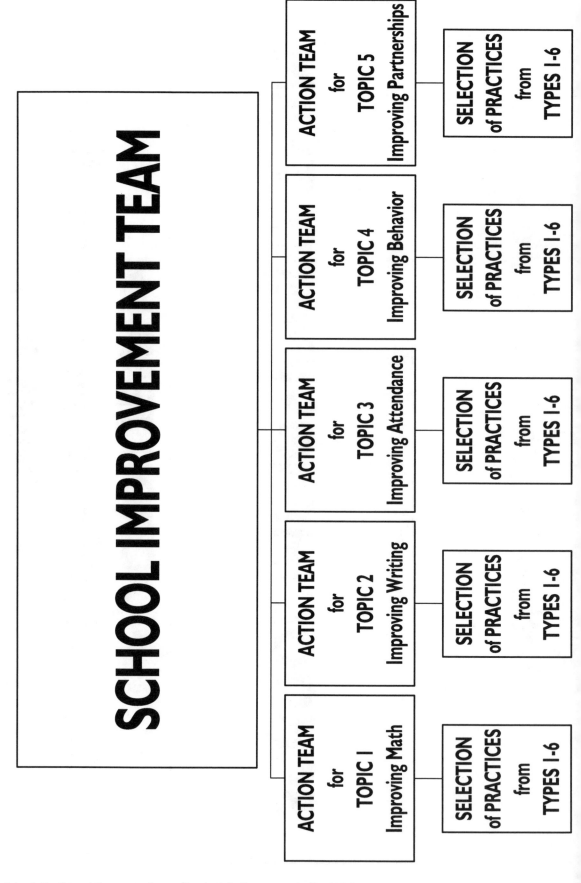

SCHOOL IMPROVEMENT TEAM

| ACTION TEAM for TOPIC 1 Improving Math | ACTION TEAM for TOPIC 2 Improving Writing | ACTION TEAM for TOPIC 3 Improving Attendance | ACTION TEAM for TOPIC 4 Improving Behavior | ACTION TEAM for TOPIC 5 Improving Partnerships |

| SELECTION of PRACTICES from TYPES 1-6 | SELECTION of PRACTICES from TYPES 1-6 | SELECTION of PRACTICES from TYPES 1-6 | SELECTION of PRACTICES from TYPES 1-6 | SELECTION of PRACTICES from TYPES 1-6 |

Members of the Action Team

FOR SCHOOL, FAMILY, AND COMMUNITY PARTNERSHIPS

How Many?   **6-12 members**

Who?   **2-3 teachers**

2-3 parents/family members, may include parent liaison, PTA officer, parents with children in different grades, families from various neighborhoods

Principal

1-2 students (in middle/high school)

1-2 other members (nurse, counselor, community members)

Terms?   **Two-to-three years (renewable) Replacements made as needed**

At least one member also serves on school improvement team or school council

Leaders?   **Chair is a member who communicates well with educators *and* families**

Other members serve as chairs or co-chairs of committees for each type of involvement

The ABCs of Action Team Leadership

The ABCs of Action Team Leadership outlines the qualities and responsibilities of the Chair or Co-chairs of the Action Team for School, Family, and Community Partnerships.

Good leadership is essential for a well-functioning Action Team. Team leaders are expected to:

A—Account for team members

B—Be ready to share leadership

C—Communicate with all partners

D—Develop good plans

E—Ensure progress on six types of involvement

F—Foster team spirit

School, Family, and Community Partnerships by J. L. Epstein et al., © 1997 Corwin Press, Inc.

A

ACCOUNT FOR TEAM MEMBERS

The Action Team Chair...

accounts for diverse members on the team who will develop and implement a program of school-family-community partnerships.

How Many?   6-12 members

Who?   2-3 teachers

2-3 parents/family members/parent liaison

Principal

1-2 students (middle/high school)

1-3 other members (school staff, community members)

At least one member also serves on the school improvement team

Term?   2-3 years (renewable)

Replacements made as needed

Leaders?   Chairperson communicates well with educators and families

Other members serve as leaders of committees for six types of involvement

Team identifies future leaders

All features are flexible to fit school needs.

B

BE READY TO SHARE LEADERSHIP

The Action Team Chair . . .

coordinates, facilitates, and manages the work of the team. Because a program of partnerships needs more than one person, the Action Team Chair:

- **Manages** the team's committee chairs, co-chairs, assistants, and helpers for the six types of involvement

- **Delegates** responsibilities for all Action Team members and other helpers

- **Schedules** meetings to ensure progress—not too few or too many

- **Develops** agendas and conducts meetings

- **Shares** responsibility and credit for the team's plans and activities

- **Prepares** the new Action Team Chair by sharing all materials, plans, and evaluations

C

COMMUNICATE WITH ALL PARTNERS

The Action Team Chair . . .

communicates with all partners about the work of the Action Team. To fulfill this responsibility, the Action Team Chair:

- Communicates with **all members of the Action Team**

- Keeps the **principal** and **school faculty** informed of progress and challenges. Helps **new faculty** and **long-term substitutes** understand and participate in the program

- Shares information with the **school improvement team** about how school, family, and community partnerships support school goals, and about the Action Team's progress

- Informs **parent organizations** about the Action Team's progress and involves them in plans and activities

- Uses newsletters and other vehicles to inform **all families** about the plans for school, family, and community partnerships, and how all are welcome to participate

- Talks with a **district facilitator** for partnerships about the school's program, progress, challenges, and help needed

D

DEVELOP GOOD PLANS

The Action Team Chair . . .

assists team members with planning and evaluation forms. These include:

- **Starting Points—at the start of the partnership program** and as needed to take an inventory of the school's current partnership practices

- **Three-Year Outline—every year or as needed** to identify long-term goals for the school's partnership program

- **One-Year Action Plan—every year** to continue, add, and improve partnership activities for all six types of involvement that are linked to the school improvement plan and goals

- **End-of-Year Evaluation—every spring** to assess the strengths and weaknesses of the school's partnership program, and to help develop the next One-Year Plan

School, Family, and Community Partnerships by J. L. Epstein et al., © 1997 Corwin Press, Inc.

E

ENSURE PROGRESS ON THE SIX TYPES OF INVOLVEMENT

The Action Team Chair . . .

oversees the work of committees conducting activities for all six types of involvement to help reach school goals

- **Moves** plans and activities along

- Periodically **revisits** the One-Year Action Plan

- **Assists** team members in overcoming or removing obstacles

- **Reaches out** to a district facilitator for school-family-community partnerships when in need of assistance

F

FOSTER TEAM SPIRIT

The Action Team Chair . . .

encourages collaboration and cooperation among team members and other partners. The team leader:

- **Respects** the ideas of **all** team members

- **Inspires** team members to work together

- **Helps** team members develop leadership skills

- **Leads by example** with enthusiasm, fairness, humor, common sense, and with organizational, communication, and problem-solving skills

- **Assists** others at the school to see the "big picture" of school, family, and community partnerships

- **Celebrates** success and has high expectations for continuous progress

  School, Family, and Community Partnerships by J. L. Epstein et al., © 1997 Corwin Press, Inc.

School-family-community partnerships grow stronger with increased levels of commitment

CAN YOU "C" THE CONNECTIONS?

1. **Care**

2. **Civility / Courtesy**

3. **Clarity**

4. **Cooperation**

5. **Collaboration**

Understanding Levels of Commitment

SCHOOL-FAMILY-COMMUNITY PARTNERSHIPS

1. *CARE.* We care about the children and each other at this school. Families feel welcome at the school. Educators feel welcome in the community.

2. *CIVILITY / COURTESY.* We respect each other at this school and recognize our shared responsibilities for children. Teachers and families talk with and listen to each other.

3. *CLARITY.* We conduct clear and useful two-way communications about school programs; children's progress, talents, and needs; community activities; and other topics important to families, students, the school, and the community.

4. *COOPERATION.* We assist each other and the students. We work together to improve the school, strengthen families, and ensure student success. We try to solve problems, and we are open to new ideas. Families, educators, and community members are comfortable working with each other.

5. *COLLABORATION.* We maintain a comprehensive program of school-family-community partnerships. We use an action team approach that enables educators, parents, students, and community members to work together over time to design, implement, and improve the six types of involvement with all families and at all grade levels. We work as partners to help students reach important goals. We encourage discussion and debate on important issues. We celebrate progress and continually plan improvements.

 School, Family, and Community Partnerships by J. L. Epstein et al., © 1997 Corwin Press, Inc.

What Questions Must Be Asked?

- Which practices of partnerships are presently strong at each grade level? Which are weak? Which should continue? Expand? Be dropped? Be added?

- Are practices coherent and coordinated or fragmented? How are families of children in Title I, special education, bilingual, and other programs part of a school-wide program of partnerships?

- Which families are you reaching and which are you not yet reaching? Which families are hardest to reach and involve, and how might they be included?

- What do *teachers* expect of families? What do *families* expect of teachers and others at school?

- What do *students* expect their families to do to help them with school life and homework? What do students want their schools to do to inform and involve their families?

- How do you want your program of school-family-community partnerships to look three years from now?

More Questions . . .

- How are your students succeeding on measures of achievement, attitudes, attendance, and other indicators of success? How might school, family, and community connections help more students reach school goals?

- What costs are associated with your school's partnership program and activities? Will small grants or other special budgets be needed? Will staff training be needed? Will money be needed for planning and development activities during summers?

- How will teachers, administrators, and parents be supported to conduct and continue work on partnerships?

- How will you evaluate the implementation and results of your efforts? What indicators, observations, and measures will be used to see how your school-family-community partnerships are progressing?

- What other questions do you have about your school's goals and plans for improving partnerships?

Do You Have . . . ?

- A *long-term plan for workshops* and other ways to provide information to all families on child and adolescent development? (Type 1)

- A *formal review of the quality of communications* with families to improve conferences, report cards, telephone communications, newsletters, and other ways of sharing information? (Type 2)

- A *coordinator for volunteers* to collect information on volunteer interests, talents, and availability, and to match volunteers with school, teacher, student, and family needs? (Type 3)

- A policy that all teachers assign *interactive homework* once a month or more that requires students to talk to someone at home about something interesting that they are learning in class? (Type 4)

- A *school-site management team* for decision making that includes parents, teachers, administrators, and students on committees and in other school improvement or problem-solving activities? (Type 5)

- An *open line of communication* with businesses, health and social service agencies, cultural institutions, and other community groups to improve school programs, strengthen families, and enrich children's learning? (Type 6)

Do You Have . . . ?

- A *room for families* where they can conduct activities as volunteers? Talk together? Confer with teachers or talk with staff? Watch tapes of workshops or films about child development? Obtain other information? This place may be called a Family Resource Center, Family Room, Parent Club, or another name.

- A *recognition program* for families who participate? For teachers who work hard to involve families? For students who help their school and families communicate? For business and community groups that work with the school and with families? For other outstanding work on partnerships?

- A *grants program* to encourage new ideas for school, family, and community partnerships? To cover costs of partnership activities?

District Leadership Roles

FOR SCHOOL-FAMILY-COMMUNITY PARTNERSHIPS

1. *WRITE A POLICY* that identifies district-level and school-level goals for school, family, and community partnerships, including all six types of involvement. Include the district's commitments to enact the policy and to assist schools to implement it.

2. *ASSIGN A FACILITATOR* (or more than one) who will oversee the district's work and assist the schools with their plans to develop programs of partnership. Provide adequate staff and resources for the district's work on partnerships.

3. *GUIDE EACH SCHOOL TO FORM AN ACTION TEAM* for School, Family, and Community Partnerships consisting of teachers, parents, and administrators.

4. *PROVIDE IN-SERVICE EDUCATION* for teachers, parents, and administrators, and TRAINING WORKSHOPS for Action Teams on the goals, practices, and planning processes for programs of partnership.

5. *HELP EACH ACTION TEAM DEVELOP A ONE-YEAR ACTION PLAN* to involve all families in their children's education. Each school's plans should link directly to its goals and objectives, and include practices for all six types of involvement.

6. *CONDUCT END-OF-YEAR CELEBRATION WORKSHOPS* to enable Action Teams to share ideas, discuss progress, solve problems, and plan ahead.

7. *PROVIDE FUNDING AND RECOGNITION PROGRAMS* for schools, including program costs for Action Teams, awards for excellent activities or improvement, and small grants for special projects.

8. *ESTABLISH A CLEARING HOUSE, NEWSLETTER, OR OTHER COMMUNICATIONS* to disseminate effective practices, ideas, materials, research, and other information that will help Action Teams improve their programs of partnership.

9. *SUPPORT RESEARCH AND EVALUATION* to learn which practices help schools produce specific results for students, parents, teachers, the school, and the community.

10. *CONDUCT OTHER DISTRICT LEADERSHIP ACTIVITIES* to build strong and permanent programs of partnership in all schools and at the district level.

State Leadership Roles

FOR SCHOOL-FAMILY-COMMUNITY PARTNERSHIPS

1. *WRITE A POLICY* that identifies state goals for school, family, and community partnerships, including all six types of involvement. Include enactments to assist districts and schools to understand and implement the policy.

2. *IDENTIFY A DEPARTMENT* for School, Family, and Community Partnerships, and provide adequate staff and resources for the coordinator.

3. *ASSIGN A COORDINATOR* who will oversee and coordinate the State Department of Education's work with families and communities, and provide technical assistance to districts and schools to develop comprehensive programs of partnership.

4. *PROVIDE IN-SERVICE EDUCATION and ANNUAL TRAINING WORKSHOPS* for district leaders, Action Teams, and other educators and parents to prepare leaders to increase their capacities to conduct programs of partnership.

5. *PROVIDE FUNDING AND RECOGNITION* to support districts and schools to develop partnerships and to reward excellence. Offer competitive grants for extra funding for special projects.

6. *CONDUCT END-OF-YEAR WORKSHOPS* to encourage regional or cross-district exchanges of good practices, ideas, and solutions to challenges of school-family-community partnerships. Or, support district-level conferences where schools share ideas and make plans to continue their programs.

7. *ESTABLISH A CLEARING HOUSE, NEWSLETTER, OR OTHER COMMUNICATIONS* to disseminate effective practices, ideas, materials, research, and other information to help districts and schools improve their programs of partnership.

8. *SUPPORT RESEARCH AND EVALUATION* to learn which practices help schools produce specific results for students, parents, teachers, schools, and communities.

9. *WORK WITH STATE COLLEGES and UNIVERSITIES* to set requirements for teaching and administrative credentials to prepare educators to understand and conduct programs of school, family, and community partnerships.

10. *WORK WITH BUSINESS and INDUSTRY* to establish flexible leave policies so parents can attend conferences at their children's schools, business-school partnerships, and volunteer programs.

5

Planning and
Evaluation Forms

This chapter provides forms to help Action Teams for School, Family, and Community Partnerships plan, implement, and evaluate their work. All Action Teams should do the following:

- Complete an inventory of present practices of school-family-community partnerships

- Outline a vision of how practices of partnership will develop and improve over three years

- Prepare a detailed one-year plan indicating how the Action Team will schedule and conduct activities to reach specific results for one school year

- Evaluate their school, family, and community partnerships program each year in order to improve practices

To complete these four tasks, you may copy and use the following forms or adapt them to match the vocabulary of local school improvement plans or other local needs.

Starting Points

This inventory helps your Action Team identify the *present* practices conducted in your school for each of the six types of involvement along with the grade levels included in the activities. The checklist helps your team think about how to increase, improve, or maintain activities for a comprehensive program of partnerships. The inventory also may be used from year to year to monitor the progress of your program.

After completing *Starting Points,* the Action Team should conduct some of the group discussions in Chapter 6 (e.g., Small Group Discussion Guide, School Goals and Results of Partnerships, and Linking

Practices With Results) to think about the school's strengths, needs, and goals for partnerships. Then, your team will be ready to draft a three-year outline and a one-year action plan for partnerships.

Three-Year Outline (Form A or B)

This broad outline asks your Action Team to set long-term goals. There are two versions of the Three-Year Outline:

- Form A (**Vision: A Comprehensive Program of Six Types of Involvement**) focuses the Action Team's attention on the goal of partnerships and the development of a comprehensive program including practices for all six types of involvement. It asks, *How should your school increase, improve, or maintain practices for each of the six types of involvement for the next three years?*

- Form B (**Reaching School Goals With School, Family, and Community Partnerships**) focuses the Action Team's attention on how partnerships link to the major goals in a school improvement plan (e.g., improving attendance, achievement in specific subjects, and safety). It asks, *Which practices of the six types of involvement will help reach the major goals your school has set for the next three years?*

You may use the Three-Year Outline (Form A or B) most appropriate for your school. To complete this outline, the Action Team should consider your school's inventory (*Starting Points*), school improvement goals, and ideas for the six types of involvement that will produce desired results. After completing the Three-Year Outline, the Action Team should discuss its vision with the school improvement team, full faculty, parent organization, students, and others who have important ideas about the directions that partnerships should take over time. Each spring, your Action Team should update the Three-Year Outline to maintain a long-term perspective.

One-Year Action Plan (Form A or B)

This form asks for specific information about the work that your Action Team will do to oversee and conduct activities for all six types of involvement to reach partnership goals or to support other goals that your school has set for the next school year. There are two versions of the One-Year Action Plan:

- Form A (**Timeline of Activities for Six Types of Involvement**) focuses the Action Team's attention on the six types of involvement. It asks, *For each type of involvement, which activi-*

ties will your school continue or add this year? (This form should be used along with Form A of the Three-Year Outline; refer to Year 1.)

- Form B (**Schedule of School, Family, and Community Partnerships to Reach School Goals**) focuses the Action Team's attention on how partnerships link to the major goals set in a school improvement plan. It asks, *Which practices of the six types of involvement will you choose to help you reach the major goals your school has set this year?* (This form should be used along with Form B of the Three-Year Outline; refer to Year 1.)

The One-Year Action Plan asks you to be clear about the dates, preparation, helpers, and results for each activity that you continue or add to your program. Your Action Team should check that the work scheduled from month to month during the year is reasonable and clearly targeted to important goals and results.

Using your inventory (*Starting Points*) and Three-Year Outline (Year 1), the Action Team should decide which activities to continue from year to year and which activities to add or improve. The Action Team also should share ideas and obtain reactions from the school community to the current One-Year Action Plan.

End-of-Year Evaluation

This form helps your Action Team think about and document the school's progress toward developing a comprehensive and effective program of school-family-community partnerships. It asks for ratings of the program and reflections about specific activities for each type of involvement. This evaluation should be completed each spring before writing the One-Year Action Plan for the next school year.

STARTING POINTS:

An Inventory of Present Practices of School-Family-Community Partnerships

Karen Clark Salinas, Joyce L. Epstein, and Mavis G. Sanders
National Network of Partnership-2000 Schools, Johns Hopkins University

This inventory will help you identify your school's present practices for each of the six types of involvement that create a comprehensive program of school, family, and community partnerships. At this time, your school may conduct all, some, or none of the activities listed. Not every activity is appropriate for every school or grade level. You may write in other activities that you conduct for each type of involvement.

The Action Team for School, Family, and Community Partnerships should complete this inventory, with input from the teachers, parents, the school improvement team, and others, as appropriate. These groups have different knowledge about all of the present practices of partnership in your school.

After you complete the inventory, you will be ready to write a Three-Year Outline and One-Year Action Plan to show how you will increase, improve, or maintain activities for each of the six types of involvement in your school. These forms are included in Chapter 5 of this handbook.

Directions: Check the activities that you conduct and circle all of the grade levels presently involved. Write in other activities for each type of involvement that your school conducts.

To assess how well each activity is implemented, add these symbols next to the check-box:
* (for very well implemented with all families), + (a good start with many families), - (needs improvement).

TYPE I – PARENTING: BASIC RESPONSIBILITIES OF FAMILIES
Assist families with parenting skills and setting home conditions to support children as students, and assist schools to understand families

At Which Grades?

☐ We sponsor parent education workshops and other courses or training for parents.　　K 1 2 3 4 5 6 7 8 9 10 11 12

☐ We provide families with information on child or adolescent development.　　K 1 2 3 4 5 6 7 8 9 10 11 12

☐ We provide families with information on developing home conditions that support learning.　　K 1 2 3 4 5 6 7 8 9 10 11 12

☐ We lend families books or tapes on parenting or videotapes of parent workshops.　　K 1 2 3 4 5 6 7 8 9 10 11 12

☐ We ask families for information about children's goals, strengths, and talents.　　K 1 2 3 4 5 6 7 8 9 10 11 12

☐ We sponsor home visiting programs or neighborhood meetings to help families understand schools and to help schools understand families.　　K 1 2 3 4 5 6 7 8 9 10 11 12

☐ _____　　K 1 2 3 4 5 6 7 8 9 10 11 12

☐ _____　　K 1 2 3 4 5 6 7 8 9 10 11 12

☐ _____　　K 1 2 3 4 5 6 7 8 9 10 11 12

☐ _____　　K 1 2 3 4 5 6 7 8 9 10 11 12

☐ _____　　K 1 2 3 4 5 6 7 8 9 10 11 12

TYPE 2 – COMMUNICATING: BASIC RESPONSIBILITIES OF SCHOOLS   At Which Grades?
Conduct effective communications from school to home and from home to school about school programs and children's progress

❑ We have formal conferences with every parent at least once a year.   K 1 2 3 4 5 6 7 8 9 10 11 12

❑ We provide language translators to assist families as needed.   K 1 2 3 4 5 6 7 8 9 10 11 12

❑ We provide clear information about report cards and how grades are earned.   K 1 2 3 4 5 6 7 8 9 10 11 12

❑ Parents pick up report cards.   K 1 2 3 4 5 6 7 8 9 10 11 12

❑ Our school newsletter includes:

    ❑ a calendar of school events   K 1 2 3 4 5 6 7 8 9 10 11 12

    ❑ student activity information   K 1 2 3 4 5 6 7 8 9 10 11 12

    ❑ curriculum and program information   K 1 2 3 4 5 6 7 8 9 10 11 12

    ❑ school volunteer information   K 1 2 3 4 5 6 7 8 9 10 11 12

    ❑ school governance information   K 1 2 3 4 5 6 7 8 9 10 11 12

    ❑ samples of student writing and artwork   K 1 2 3 4 5 6 7 8 9 10 11 12

    ❑ a column to address parents' questions   K 1 2 3 4 5 6 7 8 9 10 11 12

    ❑ recognition of students, families, and community members   K 1 2 3 4 5 6 7 8 9 10 11 12

    ❑ other _____   K 1 2 3 4 5 6 7 8 9 10 11 12

❑ We provide clear information about selecting courses, programs, and activities in this school.   K 1 2 3 4 5 6 7 8 9 10 11 12

❑ We send home folders of student work weekly or monthly for parent review and comments.   K 1 2 3 4 5 6 7 8 9 10 11 12

❑ Staff members send home positive messages about students on a regular basis.   K 1 2 3 4 5 6 7 8 9 10 11 12

❑ We notify families about student awards and recognition.   K 1 2 3 4 5 6 7 8 9 10 11 12

❑ We contact the families of students having academic or behavior problems.   K 1 2 3 4 5 6 7 8 9 10 11 12

❑ Teachers have easy access to telephones to communicate with parents during or after school.   K 1 2 3 4 5 6 7 8 9 10 11 12

❑ Parents have the telephone numbers of the school, principal, teachers and counselors.   K 1 2 3 4 5 6 7 8 9 10 11 12

❑ We have a homework hotline for students and families to hear daily assignments and messages.   K 1 2 3 4 5 6 7 8 9 10 11 12

❑ We conduct an annual survey for families to share information and concerns about students' needs and reactions to school programs.   K 1 2 3 4 5 6 7 8 9 10 11 12

❑ _____   K 1 2 3 4 5 6 7 8 9 10 11 12

❑ _____   K 1 2 3 4 5 6 7 8 9 10 11 12

❑ _____   K 1 2 3 4 5 6 7 8 9 10 11 12

❑ _____   K 1 2 3 4 5 6 7 8 9 10 11 12

❑ _____   K 1 2 3 4 5 6 7 8 9 10 11 12

❑ _____   K 1 2 3 4 5 6 7 8 9 10 11 12

TYPE 3 – VOLUNTEERING: INVOLVEMENT AT AND FOR THE SCHOOL
Organize volunteers and audiences to support the school and students

At Which Grades?

☐ We conduct an annual survey to identify interests, talents, and availability of volunteers.
K 1 2 3 4 5 6 7 8 9 10 11 12

☐ We have a parent room or family center for volunteer work, meetings, and resources for families.
K 1 2 3 4 5 6 7 8 9 10 11 12

☐ We encourage families and the community to be involved at school by:

  ☐ assisting in the classroom (e.g., tutoring, grading papers, etc.)
K 1 2 3 4 5 6 7 8 9 10 11 12

  ☐ helping on trips or at parties
K 1 2 3 4 5 6 7 8 9 10 11 12

  ☐ giving talks (e.g., careers, hobbies, etc.)
K 1 2 3 4 5 6 7 8 9 10 11 12

  ☐ checking attendance
K 1 2 3 4 5 6 7 8 9 10 11 12

  ☐ monitoring halls, or working in the library, cafeteria, or other areas
K 1 2 3 4 5 6 7 8 9 10 11 12

  ☐ leading clubs or activities
K 1 2 3 4 5 6 7 8 9 10 11 12

  ☐ other _____
K 1 2 3 4 5 6 7 8 9 10 11 12

☐ We provide ways for families to be involved at home or in the community if they cannot volunteer at school.
K 1 2 3 4 5 6 7 8 9 10 11 12

☐ We have a program to recognize our volunteers.
K 1 2 3 4 5 6 7 8 9 10 11 12

☐ We schedule plays, concerts, games, and other events at different times of the day or evening so that all parents can attend some activities.
K 1 2 3 4 5 6 7 8 9 10 11 12

☐ _____
K 1 2 3 4 5 6 7 8 9 10 11 12

☐ _____
K 1 2 3 4 5 6 7 8 9 10 11 12

☐ _____
K 1 2 3 4 5 6 7 8 9 10 11 12

☐ _____
K 1 2 3 4 5 6 7 8 9 10 11 12

TYPE 4 – LEARNING AT HOME: INVOLVEMENT IN ACADEMIC ACTIVITIES
Involve families with their children in homework and other curriculum-related activities and decisions

At Which Grades?

☐ We provide information to families on required skills in all subjects.
K 1 2 3 4 5 6 7 8 9 10 11 12

☐ We provide information to families on how to monitor and discuss schoolwork at home.
K 1 2 3 4 5 6 7 8 9 10 11 12

☐ We provide information on how to assist students with skills that they need to improve.
K 1 2 3 4 5 6 7 8 9 10 11 12

☐ We have a regular schedule of interactive homework that requires students to demonstrate and discuss what they are learning with a family member.
K 1 2 3 4 5 6 7 8 9 10 11 12

☐ We ask parents to listen to their child read or to read aloud with their child.
K 1 2 3 4 5 6 7 8 9 10 11 12

☐ We provide calendars with daily or weekly activities for families to do at home and in the community.
K 1 2 3 4 5 6 7 8 9 10 11 12

☐ We help families help students set academic goals, select courses and programs, and plan for college or work.
K 1 2 3 4 5 6 7 8 9 10 11 12

☐ _____
K 1 2 3 4 5 6 7 8 9 10 11 12

☐ _____
K 1 2 3 4 5 6 7 8 9 10 11 12

☐ _____
K 1 2 3 4 5 6 7 8 9 10 11 12

☐ _____
K 1 2 3 4 5 6 7 8 9 10 11 12

TYPE 5 – DECISION MAKING: PARTICIPATION AND LEADERSHIP
At Which Grades?

Include families as participants in school decisions, and develop parent leaders and representatives

❑ We have an active PTA, PTO, or other parent organization.　K 1 2 3 4 5 6 7 8 9 10 11 12

❑ Parents are represented on the school's advisory council, improvement team, or other committees.　K 1 2 3 4 5 6 7 8 9 10 11 12

❑ We have an Action Team for School, Family, and Community Partnerships to develop a program with practices for all six types of involvement.　K 1 2 3 4 5 6 7 8 9 10 11 12

❑ Parents are represented on district-level advisory councils and committees.　K 1 2 3 4 5 6 7 8 9 10 11 12

❑ We provide information on school or local elections for school representatives.　K 1 2 3 4 5 6 7 8 9 10 11 12

❑ We develop formal networks to link all families with their parent representatives.　K 1 2 3 4 5 6 7 8 9 10 11 12

❑ We involve parents in selecting school staff.　K 1 2 3 4 5 6 7 8 9 10 11 12

❑ We involve parents in revising school/district curricula.　K 1 2 3 4 5 6 7 8 9 10 11 12

❑ _____　K 1 2 3 4 5 6 7 8 9 10 11 12

❑ _____　K 1 2 3 4 5 6 7 8 9 10 11 12

❑ _____　K 1 2 3 4 5 6 7 8 9 10 11 12

❑ _____　K 1 2 3 4 5 6 7 8 9 10 11 12

TYPE 6 – COLLABORATING WITH THE COMMUNITY
At Which Grades?

Coordinate resources and services _from_ the community for families, students, and the school, and provide services to the community.

❑ We provide a community resource directory for parents and students with information on community agencies, programs, and services.　K 1 2 3 4 5 6 7 8 9 10 11 12

❑ We provide information on community activities that link to learning skills and talents, including summer programs for students.　K 1 2 3 4 5 6 7 8 9 10 11 12

❑ We work with local businesses, industries, and community organizations on programs to enhance student skills.　K 1 2 3 4 5 6 7 8 9 10 11 12

❑ We offer after-school programs for students, with support from community businesses, agencies, or volunteers.　K 1 2 3 4 5 6 7 8 9 10 11 12

❑ We sponsor intergenerational programs with local senior citizen groups.　K 1 2 3 4 5 6 7 8 9 10 11 12

❑ We provide "one-stop" shopping for family services through partnerships of school, counseling, health, recreation, job training, and other agencies.　K 1 2 3 4 5 6 7 8 9 10 11 12

❑ We organize service _to_ the community by students, families, and schools.　K 1 2 3 4 5 6 7 8 9 10 11 12

❑ We include alumni in school programs for students.　K 1 2 3 4 5 6 7 8 9 10 11 12

❑ Our school building is open for use by the community after school hours.　K 1 2 3 4 5 6 7 8 9 10 11 12

❑ _____　K 1 2 3 4 5 6 7 8 9 10 11 12

❑ _____　K 1 2 3 4 5 6 7 8 9 10 11 12

❑ _____　K 1 2 3 4 5 6 7 8 9 10 11 12

❑ _____　K 1 2 3 4 5 6 7 8 9 10 11 12

Three-Year Outline From _____ To _____

VISION: A COMPREHENSIVE PROGRAM OF SIX TYPES OF INVOLVEMENT

School _____

Outline the activities that might help your school improve all six types of involvement over the next three years. What steps might your Action Team take in Year 1, Year 2, and Year 3 to improve Parenting, Communicating, Volunteering, Learning at Home, Decision Making, and Collaborating With the Community? (Use this form *after* completing **Starting Points: An Inventory of Present Practices** and *before* completing the **One-Year Action Plan—Form A.**)

Type 1—PARENTING: Assist families with parenting skills, family support, understanding child and adolescent development, and setting home conditions to support learning at each age and grade level. Obtain information from families to help schools understand children's strengths, talents, and needs, and families' backgrounds, cultures, and goals for their children.

Vision: What is your Action Team's broad goal for improving **Type 1—Parenting** over the next 3 years? _____

Which ACTIVITIES might you conduct over 3 years to reach your vision for Type 1—Parenting?

Year 1 _____

Year 2 _____

Year 3 _____

Type 2—Communicating: Communicate with families about school programs and student progress using school-to-home and home-to-school communications. Create two-way channels so that families can easily contact teachers and administrators.

Vision: What is your Action Team's broad goal for improving **Type 2—Communicating** over the next 3 years? _____

Which ACTIVITIES might you conduct over 3 years to reach your vision for Type 2—Communicating?

Year 1 _____

Year 2 _____

Year 3 _____

126

School, Family, and Community Partnerships by J. L. Epstein et al., © 1997 Corwin Press, Inc.
Photocopying permissible for local school use only.

Type 3—VOLUNTEERING: Improve recruitment, training, activities, and schedules to involve families as volunteers and audiences at the school or in other locations to support students and the school's programs.

VISION: What is your Action Team's broad goal for improving Type 3—Volunteering over the next 3 years? _____

_____

Which ACTIVITIES might you conduct over 3 years to reach your vision for Type 3—Volunteering?

Year 1 _____

Year 2 _____

Year 3 _____

Type 4—LEARNING AT HOME: Involve families with their children in academic learning activities at home including homework, goal setting, and other curriculum-related activities and decisions.

Vision: What is your Action Team's broad goal for improving Type 4—Learning at Home over the next 3 years? _____

_____

Which ACTIVITIES might you conduct over 3 years to reach your vision for Type 4—Learning at Home?

Year 1 _____

Year 2 _____

Year 3 _____

Type 5—DECISION MAKING: Include families as participants in school decisions, governance, and advocacy activities through PTA/PTO, committees, councils, and other parent organizations. Assist family representatives to obtain information from and give information to those they represent.

VISION: What is your Action Team's broad goal for improving Type 5—Decision Making over the next 3 years? ___

Which ACTIVITIES might you conduct over 3 years to reach your vision for Type 5—Decision Making?

Year 1 _____

_____

Year 2 _____

_____

Year 3 _____

_____

Type 6—COLLABORATING WITH THE COMMUNITY: Coordinate the work and resources of community businesses, agencies, cultural and civic organizations, and other groups to strengthen school programs, family practices, and student learning and development. Enable students, staff, and families to contribute service to the community.

VISION: What is your Action Team's broad goal for improving Type 6—Collaborating With the Community over the next 3 years? _____

Which ACTIVITIES might you conduct over 3 years to reach your vision for Type 6—Collaborating With the Community?

Year 1 _____

_____

Year 2 _____

_____

Year 3 _____

_____

128

School _____   **FORM B**

Three-Year Outline From _____ To _____

REACHING SCHOOL GOALS WITH SCHOOL, FAMILY, AND COMMUNITY PARTNERSHIPS

- List **ONE MAJOR GOAL** for your school on each page. (Make copies of this page for each of your school's major goals.)
- Next, list **specific, measurable results for this goal for Year 1, Year 2, and Year 3.**
- Finally, list activities for **school-family-community partnerships** that will help reach the desired results for THIS goal in Years 1, 2, and 3.

ONE MAJOR GOAL: _____

_____

DESIRED RESULTS FOR THIS GOAL by the end of **YEAR 1**: _____

_____

Links with School-Family-Community Partnerships:
Which practices of partnership will help reach the desired results for THIS goal in **Year 1?**

Type 1–Parenting: _____

Type 2–Communicating: _____

Type 3–Volunteering: _____

Type 4–Learning at Home: _____

Type 5–Decision Making: _____

Type 6–Collaborating With the Community: _____

DESIRED RESULTS FOR THIS GOAL by the end of **YEAR 2**: _____

_____

Links with School-Family-Community Partnerships:
Which practices of partnership will help reach the desired results for THIS goal in **Year 2?**

Type 1–Parenting: _____

Type 2–Communicating: _____

Type 3–Volunteering: _____

Type 4–Learning at Home: _____

Type 5–Decision Making: _____

Type 6–Collaborating With the Community: _____

DESIRED RESULTS FOR THIS GOAL by the end of **YEAR 3**: _____

_____

Links with School-Family-Community Partnerships:
Which practices of partnership will help reach the desired results for THIS goal in **Year 3?**

Type 1–Parenting: _____

Type 2–Communicating: _____

Type 3–Volunteering: _____

Type 4–Learning at Home: _____

Type 5–Decision Making: _____

Type 6–Collaborating With the Community: _____

One-Year Action Plan

TIME-LINE OF ACTIVITIES FOR SIX TYPES OF INVOLVEMENT

School Year: _____

For your One-Year Action Plan, the Action Team for School, Family, and Community Partnerships should consider the activities that are *presently conducted at the school and that will be continued, as well as new activities that will strengthen all six types of involvement.*

- See *Starting Points: An Inventory of Present Practices.*
- See *Three-Year Outline* (Form A) to develop a long-term vision of partnerships before completing this One-Year Action Plan.

Type I–PARENTING: Assist families with parenting skills, family support, understanding child and adolescent development, and setting home conditions to support learning at each age and grade level. Obtain information from families to help schools understand children's strengths, talents, and needs, and families' backgrounds, cultures, and goals for their children.

Type I–Committee Chair or Co-Chairs: _____

TYPE I ACTIVITY (continuing or new)	Date of Activity	Grade Level(s)	What Needs To Be Done for Activity & When?	Persons in Charge and Helping	What RESULTS & How Measured?

Any extra funds, supplies, or resources needed for these activities? _____

You may add pages to show more activities that support THIS type of involvement or to provide detailed plans for the work that must be done THIS YEAR.

School _____

Type 2—COMMUNICATING: Communicate with families about school programs and student progress using school-to-home and home-to-school communications. Create two-way channels so that families can easily contact teachers and administrators.

Type 2—Committee Chair or Co-Chairs: _____

TYPE 2 ACTIVITY (continuing or new)	Date of Activity	Grade Level(s)	What Needs To Be Done for Activity & When?	Persons in Charge and Helping	What RESULTS & How Measured?

Any extra funds, supplies, or resources needed for these activities? _____

You may add pages to show more activities that support THIS type of involvement or to provide detailed plans for the work that must be done THIS YEAR.

Type 3—VOLUNTEERING: Improve recruitment, training, activities, and schedules to involve families as volunteers and audiences at the school or in other locations to support students and the school's programs.

Type 3—Committee Chair or Co-Chairs: _____

TYPE 3 ACTIVITY (continuing or new)	Date of Activity	Grade Level(s)	What Needs To Be Done for Activity & When?	Persons in Charge and Helping	What RESULTS & How Measured?

Any extra funds, supplies, or resources needed for these activities? _____

You may add pages to show more activities that support THIS type of involvement or to provide detailed plans for the work that must be done THIS YEAR.

Type 4–LEARNING AT HOME: Involve families with their children in academic learning activities at home including homework, goal setting, and other curriculum-related activities and decisions.

Type 4–Committee Chair or Co-Chairs: _____

TYPE 4 ACTIVITY (continuing or new)	Date of Activity	Grade Level(s)	What Needs To Be Done for Activity & When?	Persons in Charge and Helping	What RESULTS & How Measured?

Any extra funds, supplies, or resources needed for these activities? _____

You may add pages to show more activities that support THIS type of involvement or to provide detailed plans for the work that must be done THIS YEAR.

Type 5–DECISION MAKING: Include families as participants in school decisions, governance, and advocacy activities through PTA/PTO, committees, councils, and other parent organizations. Assist family representatives to obtain information from and give information to those they represent.

Type 5–Committee Chair or Co-Chairs: _____

TYPE 5 ACTIVITY (continuing or new)	Date of Activity	Grade Level(s)	What Needs To Be Done for Activity & When?	Persons in Charge and Helping	What RESULTS & How Measured?

Any extra funds, supplies, or resources needed for these activities? _____

You may add pages to show more activities that support THIS type of involvement or to provide detailed plans for the work that must be done THIS YEAR.

Type 6—COLLABORATING WITH THE COMMUNITY: Coordinate the work and resources of community businesses, agencies, cultural, civic, and other organizations to strengthen school programs, family practices, and student learning and development. Enable students, staff, and families to contribute service to the community.

Type 6—Committee Chair or Co-Chairs: _____

TYPE 6 ACTIVITY (continuing or new)	Date of Activity	Grade Level(s)	What Needs To Be Done for Activity & When?	Persons in Charge and Helping	What RESULTS & How Measured?

Any extra funds, supplies, or resources needed for these activities? _____

You may add pages to show more activities that support THIS type of involvement or to provide detailed plans for the work that must be done THIS YEAR.

One-Year Action Plan

School _____

SCHEDULE OF SCHOOL, FAMILY, AND COMMUNITY PARTNERSHIPS TO REACH SCHOOL GOALS

School Year: _____

- List ONE of your school's major goals for the school year. (Make copies of this page for each of your school's major goals.)
- List the specific, measurable results that will show you have reached THIS goal.

ONE Major Goal: _____

Desired results for THIS goal: _____

How will you measure these results? _____

- Which practices of school-family-community partnerships will help you reach THIS goal? (Choose activities from more than one type of involvement.)
- How will you organize and schedule activities for the six types of involvement that support THIS goal?

ACTIVITY (continuing or new)	Type (1-6)	Date of Activity	Grade Level(s)	What Needs to Be Done for Activity & When?	Persons in Charge and Helping

Any extra funds, supplies, or resources needed for these activities? _____

You may add pages to show more activities that support THIS goal or to provide detailed plans for the work that must be done THIS YEAR.

School Name _____   School Year _____

End-of-Year Evaluation

SCHOOL-FAMILY-COMMUNITY PARTNERSHIPS

This annual report helps your school evaluate its progress in developing a comprehensive program of school-family-community partnerships. The report contains one set of general questions and one page for each of the six types of involvement.

The entire Action Team for School, Family, and Community Partnerships may complete the general questions on the first page. The chair or co-chairs who oversee committees on each of the six types of involvement may complete one page about the type of involvement for which they are responsible. Add pages if you need more space to document your progress.

This report should assist the Action Team with its One-Year Action Plan for the next school year.

General Questions:

1. What has changed most in the past year as a result of your work on school-family-community partnerships? _____

   _____

2. Overall, how would you rate the quality of your school's program of school-family-community partnerships? _____

   _____

   Our school's partnership program is:
   _____ a. **Poor**—Not well developed; needs a great deal of work
   _____ b. **Fair**—Implemented but needs improvement and expansion
   _____ c. **Good**—Well developed; covers all six types of involvement and addresses the needs of most families at most grade levels
   _____ d. **Excellent**—Well developed and implemented; covers all six types of involvement and addresses the needs of all families at all grade levels

Action Team members for this school year	Position (e.g., teacher, parent, etc.)	Responsible for or helping with which type of involvement?
1. _____	_____	_____
2. _____	_____	_____
3. _____	_____	_____
4. _____	_____	_____
5. _____	_____	_____
6. _____	_____	_____
7. _____	_____	_____
8. _____	_____	_____
9. _____	_____	_____
10. _____	_____	_____
11. _____	_____	_____
12. _____	_____	_____

Evaluation of Type 1—PARENTING Activities: Type 1 activities help families understand their children's development and improve their parenting skills, and help schools understand their students' families.

1. List all Type 1—PARENTING activities that your Action Team implemented or improved during this school year (e.g., workshops on parenting skills; bi-weekly GED classes; clothing swap; food bank; etc.).

   _____

   _____

   _____

2. Overall, how would you rate the quality of all Type 1 activities that your school presently conducts? (Check one)

   This school's Type 1—PARENTING activities are:

   _____ a. Poor—Not well developed; need a great deal of work

   _____ b. Fair—Implemented, but need improvement and expansion

   _____ c. Good—Well developed and reach most families at most grade levels

   _____ d. Excellent—Well developed and implemented; reach all families at all grade levels, and meet other major challenges

3. Select one Type 1 activity that you want to describe in detail (i.e., an activity that reflects your school's best effort this year), and answer the following questions.

   Which Type 1 activity will you describe? _____

   About how many were involved?   # of families _____   # of teachers _____

                                        # of students _____   # of others _____

   Which grade levels were involved? _____

   What was the main goal of this activity? _____

   _____

How well was the activity implemented this year? Was it a new initiative or an improvement of an existing practice?

   _____

   _____

   _____

What result(s) did this activity produce this year for students, teachers, parents, and/or the community? How were the results measured?

   _____

   _____

   _____

What might be done to make this activity even more successful next year? Were there parents, teachers, or students who were not involved? How might they be involved in the future? Could other aspects of the practice be improved? Explain.

   _____

   _____

   _____

   _____

Evaluation of Type 2—COMMUNICATING Activities: Type 2 activities include school-to-home and home-to-school communications about school and classroom programs and children's progress.

1. List all **Type 2—COMMUNICATING** activities that your Action Team implemented or improved during this school year (e.g., newsletter; parent-teacher conferences; positive telephone calls; etc.).

_____

_____

_____

2. Overall, how would you rate the quality of all **Type 2** activities that your school presently conducts? (Check one)

   This school's **Type 2—COMMUNICATING** activities are:

   _____ a. **Poor**—Not well developed; need a great deal of work

   _____ b. **Fair**—Implemented, but need improvement and expansion

   _____ c. **Good**—Well developed and reach most families at most grade levels

   _____ d. **Excellent**—Well developed and implemented; reach all families at all grade levels, and meet other major challenges

3. Select _one Type 2 activity that you want to describe in detail (i.e., an activity that reflects your school's best effort this year), and answer the following questions._

   Which **Type 2** activity will you describe? _____

   About how many were involved?　　# of families _____　　# of teachers _____

   　　　　　　　　　　　　　　　　　　　# of students _____　　# of others _____

   Which grade levels were involved? _____

   What was the main goal of this activity? _____

   _____

   How well was the activity implemented this year? Was it a new initiative or an improvement of an existing practice?

   _____

   _____

   _____

   What result(s) did this activity produce this year for students, teachers, parents, and/or the community? How were the results measured?

   _____

   _____

   _____

   What might be done to make this activity even more successful next year? Were there parents, teachers, or students who were _not involved? How might they be involved in the future? Could other aspects of the practice be improved? Explain_.

   _____

   _____

   _____

   _____

Evaluation of Type 3—VOLUNTEERING Activities: Type 3 activities enable families to give their time and talents to support schools, teachers, and children. Volunteers may conduct activities at school, at home, or in the community.

1. List all **Type 3—VOLUNTEERING** activities that your Action Team implemented or improved during this school year (e.g., volunteer workshops; volunteer programs for tutors, hall monitors, office assistants; etc.).

   _____
   _____
   _____

2. Overall, how would you rate the quality of all **Type 3** activities that your school presently conducts? (Check one)

   This school's **Type 3—VOLUNTEERING** activities are:

   _____ a. **Poor**—Not well developed; need a great deal of work

   _____ b. **Fair**—Implemented, but need improvement and expansion

   _____ c. **Good**—Well developed and reach most families at most grade levels

   _____ d. **Excellent**—Well developed and implemented; reach all families at all grade levels, and meet other major challenges

3. Select *one* Type 3 activity that you want to describe in detail (i.e., an activity that reflects your school's best effort this year), and answer the following questions.

   Which Type 3 activity will you describe? _____

   About how many were involved?   # of families _____   # of teachers _____
                                     # of students _____   # of others _____

   Which grade levels were involved? _____

   What was the main goal of this activity? _____
   _____

   How well was the activity implemented this year? Was it a new initiative or an improvement of an existing practice?

   _____
   _____
   _____

   What result(s) did this activity produce this year for students, teachers, parents, and/or the community? How were the results measured?

   _____
   _____
   _____

   What might be done to make this activity even more successful next year? Were there parents, teachers, or students who were *not* involved? How might they be involved in the future? Could other aspects of the practice be improved? Explain.

   _____
   _____
   _____
   _____

Evaluation of Type 4—LEARNING AT HOME Activities: Type 4 activities provide information and ideas to families about the academic work their children do in class, how to help their children with homework, and other curriculum-related activities and decisions.

1. List all **Type 4—LEARNING AT HOME** activities that your Action Team implemented or improved during this school year (e.g., interactive homework; summer learning packets; reading at home program; etc.).

_____

_____

_____

2. Overall, how would you rate the quality of all **Type 4** activities that your school presently conducts? (Check one)

   This school's **Type 4—LEARNING AT HOME** activities are:

   _____ a. **Poor**—Not well developed; need a great deal of work
   _____ b. **Fair**—Implemented, but need improvement and expansion
   _____ c. **Good**—Well developed and reach most families at most grade levels
   _____ d. **Excellent**—Well developed and implemented; reach all families at all grade levels, and meet other major challenges

3. Select *one* Type 4 activity that you want to describe in detail (i.e., an activity that reflects your school's best effort this year), and answer the following questions.

   Which **Type 4** activity will you describe? _____

   About how many were involved?   # of families _____   # of teachers _____
                                    # of students _____   # of others _____

   Which grade levels were involved? _____

   What was the main goal of this activity? _____

   _____

   How well was the activity implemented this year? Was it a new initiative or an improvement of an existing practice?

   _____

   _____

   _____

   What result(s) did this activity produce this year for students, teachers, parents, and/or the community? How were the results measured?

   _____

   _____

   _____

   What might be done to make this activity even more successful next year? Were there parents, teachers, or students who were *not* involved? How might they be involved in the future? Could other aspects of the practice be improved? Explain.

   _____

   _____

   _____

   _____

Evaluation of Type 5—DECISION-MAKING Activities: Type 5 activities enable families to participate in decisions about school programs that affect their own and other children.

1. List all **Type 5—DECISION-MAKING** activities that your Action Team implemented or improved during this school year (e.g., leadership workshops; family representatives on a school improvement team, school council, school action team, PTA; etc.).

   _____

   _____

   _____

2. Overall, how would you rate the quality of all **Type 5** activities that your school presently conducts? (Check one)

   This school's **Type 5—DECISION MAKING** activities are:

   _____   a. **Poor**—Not well developed; need a great deal of work

   _____   b. **Fair**—Implemented, but need improvement and expansion

   _____   c. **Good**—Well developed and reach most families at most grade levels

   _____   d. **Excellent**—Well developed and implemented; reach all families at all grade levels, and meet other major challenges

3. Select *one* Type 5 activity that you want to describe in detail (i.e., an activity that reflects your school's best effort this year), and answer the following questions.

   Which Type 5 activity will you describe? _____

   About how many were involved?   # of families _____   # of teachers _____
                                        # of students _____   # of others _____

   Which grade levels were involved? _____

   What was the main goal of this activity? _____

   _____

   How well was the activity implemented this year? Was it a new initiative or an improvement of an existing practice?

   _____

   _____

   _____

   What result(s) did this activity produce this year for students, teachers, parents, and/or the community? How were the results measured?

   _____

   _____

   _____

   What might be done to make this activity even more successful next year? Were there parents, teachers, or students who were *not* involved? How might they be involved in the future? Could other aspects of the practice be improved? Explain.

   _____

   _____

   _____

   _____

Evaluation of Type 6—COLLABORATING WITH THE COMMUNITY Activities: Type 6 activities facilitate cooperation and collaboration among schools, families, and community groups, organizations, agencies and individuals.

1. List all **Type 6—COLLABORATING WITH THE COMMUNITY** activities that your Action Team implemented or improved during this school year (e.g., business partnerships; community resource handbook; integrated services; etc.).

_____

_____

_____

2. Overall, how would you rate the quality of all **Type 6** activities that your school presently conducts? (Check one)

   This school's **Type 6—COLLABORATING WITH THE COMMUNITY** activities are:

   _____ a. **Poor**—Not well developed; need a great deal of work
   _____ b. **Fair**—Implemented, but need improvement and expansion
   _____ c. **Good**—Well developed and reach most families at most grade levels
   _____ d. **Excellent**—Well developed and implemented; reach all families at all grade levels, and meet other major challenges

3. Select _one_ **Type 6** activity that you want to describe in detail (i.e., an activity that reflects your school's best effort this year), and answer the following questions.

   Which **Type 6** activity will you describe? _____

   About how many were involved?   # of families _____   # of teachers _____
                                      # of students _____   # of others _____

   Which grade levels were involved? _____

   What was the main goal of this activity? _____
   _____

   How well was the activity implemented this year? Was it a new initiative or an improvement of an existing practice?

   _____

   _____

   What result(s) did this activity produce this year for students, teachers, parents, and/or the community? How were the results measured?

   _____

   _____

   What might be done to make this activity even more successful next year? Were there parents, teachers, or students who were _not_ involved? How might they be involved in the future? Could other aspects of the practice be improved? Explain.

   _____

   _____

   _____

   _____

6

Other Helpful Forms
for Developing Programs
of Partnership

This chapter contains various forms that facilitate thinking, sharing, planning, and developing partnerships. Schools may use or adapt the following forms to meet their needs:

- **What Do Facilitators Do?** This form outlines the many ways that district or state facilitators help the schools and Action Teams with which they work.

- **Checklist: Are You Ready?** This checklist helps your Action Team keep track of important actions and decisions that ensure progress in programs of partnership.

- **Who Are the Members of the Action Team for School, Family, and Community Partnerships?** This form asks for a list of the members of the Action Team for School, Family, and Community Partnerships, how they may be contacted, and the strengths they bring to the Action Team.

- **Small Group Discussion Guide.** The Small Group Discussion Guide asks Action Teams for information about presently successful practices, challenges that were met, and ideas for improving practices of the six types of involvement.

- **School Goals and Results of Partnerships.** This form helps Action Teams focus on the major goals that have been set for students and the school and specific practices of the six types of involvement that will help produce desired results.

- **Linking Practices With Results.** This form encourages Action Teams to think more about the specific results that might be promoted by specific practices for each of the six types of involvement.

- **Summary of School Visits.** This form helps district or state facilitators record information about the visits they make to schools.

- **Gathering Good Ideas.** This form helps educators and parents listen and learn from others' reports and exhibits on promising practices. It can be used to take notes on activities that may be adopted or adapted to strengthen partnerships in their schools.

- **Transitions: Involving Families When Students Move to New Schools.** This form enables Action Teams to plan activities to help students and their families make successful transitions to new schools.

- **Sample Pledges or Contracts.** Some schools use pledge forms or "contracts" that list the basic responsibilities of students, parents, and educators. Examples are provided of parallel forms for students, parents, and teachers that support and encourage partnership activities.

What Do Facilitators Do?

HOW DISTRICT-LEVEL FACILITATORS HELP *EVERY SCHOOL* DEVELOP A STRONG PROGRAM OF SCHOOL-FAMILY-COMMUNITY PARTNERSHIPS

Facilitators help their schools set a course, stay on course, reach their goals, share ideas with one another, and continue their plans and programs. The facilitators conduct training, planning, networking, and technical assistance activities, including doing the following:

- Help the schools establish Action Teams for School, Family, and Community partnerships
- Provide training to the Action Teams to help them understand the framework of the six types of involvement
- Help the Action Teams use the framework to develop *three-year outlines* for improving partnerships
- Help the Action Teams use the framework to write *one-year action plans* for improving partnerships
- Help the schools tailor their practices of partnership to help reach specific school improvement goals, such as improving attendance, achievement, behavior, school climate, and family involvement
- Help the schools focus on meeting specific challenges that affect the success of their practices of partnership
- Help the schools assess the results of their practices of partnership in activity-based and annual evaluations
- Meet with the Action Team leaders and team members at least once a month and more as requested or needed
- Conduct quarterly cluster meetings that bring groups of schools together to share best practices
- Meet individually with principals to clarify the work of the facilitator and how the principal will support the work of the Action Team for School, Family, and Community Partnerships
- Conduct end-of-year workshops to celebrate progress, share problems, and continue planning
- Conduct other activities to assist the Action Teams for School, Family, and Community Partnerships with their work such as presentations to staffs, families, school improvement teams, or others

The facilitators also conduct other *meetings and presentations*:

- Meet with the district administrators to discuss their expectations for the program and to clarify how they will encourage principals to support the work of their schools' Action Teams for School, Family, and Community Partnerships
- Make presentations to groups of principals, superintendents, district leaders, parents, or to other groups interested in improving partnerships

The success of a program of partnerships depends on the work of the Action Team and others at each school, responsive technical assistance from the facilitator, support from the school principal, and support from district and state leaders.

Checklist: Are You Ready?

GETTING STARTED WITH AN ACTION TEAM
FOR SCHOOL, FAMILY, AND COMMUNITY PARTNERSHIPS

The chair of the Action Team for School, Family, and Community Partnerships will guide these activities.

CHECK (✔) WHEN YOU HAVE COMPLETED THE FOLLOWING:

❏ **Selected the members of the Action Team for School, Family, and Community Partnerships** including six to twelve members, with teachers, parents, principal, and others selected for their interest in and commitment to positive family-school-community connections

❏ **Identified the chair and co-chair of the Action Team for School, Family, and Community Partnerships**

❏ **Identified the chair or co-chairs of committees for each of the six types of involvement**

❏ **Decided how often the Action Team for School, Family, and Community Partnerships will link and report to the school improvement team,** school council, or other decision-making body or office, and established a schedule for these connections

❏ **Decided how often the Action Team for School, Family, and Community Partnerships will link and report to the whole faculty, parent organizations**, and school community, and established a schedule for these connections

❏ **Completed an inventory of *present* practices** at all grade levels for each of the six types of involvement. Discussed the inventory with teachers, parents, students, and others and obtained their ideas about partnership activities that need to be maintained, improved, and added (See *Starting Points*.)

❏ **Completed a Three-Year Outline** of broad goals for each of the six types of involvement to show how the school's program of partnerships will develop over three years

❏ **Completed a One-Year Action Plan** specifying activities for each of the six types of involvement, who is responsible for implementing them, when they will be conducted, and what results are expected

❏ **Established a reasonable schedule of meetings of the Action Team** (e.g., monthly or every other month), and a reasonable schedule of meetings of the committees that will work on each of the six types of involvement or other school improvement goals

❏ **Designed and scheduled a "kickoff" activity** to effectively convey the message that the school is a "partnership place," and that the Action Team for School, Family, and Community Partnerships (or its local name) will be working with *all* teachers, families, students, and others to improve school-family-community connections as a permanent part of the school program and school improvement

Who Are the Members of the Action Team for School, Family, and Community Partnerships?

The Action Team for School, Family, and Community Partnerships should have at least 6 but no more than 12 members. Among these should be two or three teachers from different grade levels, at least two or three parents whose children are at different grade levels, and the principal or another administrator. Other members may include one or two students in the upper grades, a school nurse, counselor, social worker, community representative, or others dedicated to maintaining good partnerships. The family members may include a Parent Liaison, an officer of the parent organization (PTA/PTO), representatives of the various neighborhoods served by the school, or others committed to working together to develop positive partnerships.

Diverse membership ensures that partnership activities take into account the various needs, interests, and talents of teachers, parents, students, and the school.

Action Team members should be selected to serve two-year or three-year (renewable) terms. Each year, replacements must be made for teachers, parents, or other members who leave the school or whose terms have ended. New members must be oriented to the work that was completed and planned.

The chair of the Action Team may be any member who not only has the respect of the other members but has good communication skills and an understanding of the partnership approach. The chair or one member of the Action Team should also serve on the school improvement team, school council, or other such body, if one exists. Other members of the Action Team serve as chairs or co-chairs of committees for each type of involvement.

The following form—**Who Are the Members of the Action Team for School, Family, and Community Partnerships?**—should be completed each year to identify the continuing and new members and their responsibilities. You can use this form as an "ice breaker" to help members meet each other and share the talents and interests they bring to the Action Team.

Who Are the Members of the Action Team
for School, Family, and Community Partnerships?

SCHOOL YEAR_____

What skills, talents, or experiences do members bring to the Action Team for School, Family, and Community Partnerships? For example, does someone have art, computer, financial, writing, or teaching talents? Contacts with community groups and organizations? Or other interests that might make him/her well suited to be a chair or co-chair for one of the six types of involvement?

List the names, addresses, and positions (teacher, parent, administrator, student, or other) of the six to twelve members of your Action Team for School, Family, and Community Partnerships. Discuss and note the strengths and talents each one brings to the Action Team.

Name: _____ Position: _____ Telephone: _____

Address: _____ Best Time to Call: _____

Strengths/Talents:_____

Name: _____ Position: _____ Telephone: _____

Address: _____ Best Time to Call: _____

Strengths/Talents:_____

Name: _____ Position: _____ Telephone: _____

Address: _____ Best Time to Call: _____

Strengths/Talents:_____

Name: _____ Position: _____ Telephone: _____

Address: _____ Best Time to Call: _____

Strengths/Talents:_____

Name: _____ Position: _____ Telephone: _____

Address: _____ Best Time to Call: _____

Strengths/Talents:_____

Name: _____ Position: _____ Telephone: _____

Address: _____ Best Time to Call: _____

Strengths/Talents:_____

Name: _____ Position: _____ Telephone: _____

Address: _____ Best Time to Call: _____

Strengths/Talents: _____

Name: _____ Position: _____ Telephone: _____

Address: _____ Best Time to Call: _____

Strengths/Talents: _____

Name: _____ Position: _____ Telephone: _____

Address: _____ Best Time to Call: _____

Strengths/Talents: _____

Name: _____ Position: _____ Telephone: _____

Address: _____ Best Time to Call: _____

Strengths/Talents: _____

Name: _____ Position: _____ Telephone: _____

Address: _____ Best Time to Call: _____

Strengths/Talents: _____

Name: _____ Position: _____ Telephone: _____

Address: _____

Strengths/Talents: _____

LEADERS THIS YEAR

Chair of Action Team: _____ Co-Chair of Action Team: _____

Chair/Co-Chair of Type 1: _____ Chair/Co-Chair of Type 4: _____

Chair/Co-Chair of Type 2: _____ Chair/Co-Chair of Type 5: _____

Chair/Co-Chair of Type 3: _____ Chair/Co-Chair of Type 6: _____

Other Leaders (list roles): _____

Small Group Discussion Guide

The Small Group Discussion Guide asks for information about a presently successful practice of school-family-community partnerships; a challenge that was met and solved in the past to involve families; ideas about the families who are presently hardest to reach; and ideas for improving practices for the six types of involvement to address major challenges.

The Discussion Guide should be used after completing *Starting Points: An Inventory of Present Practices*. It gives Action Teams an opportunity to talk about some of the challenges they must meet to develop a full and inclusive program of school-family-community partnerships. About two hours should be scheduled for an Action Team meeting to discuss the questions in the Discussion Guide.

The Small Group Discussion Guide also may be used in a Training Workshop after the facilitator presents information on the challenges for the six types of involvement. We recommend using **Question 2— Jumping Hurdles** as a one-page activity for workshop attendees (see Training Workshop Agendas in Chapter 3).

Small Group Discussion Guide

_____

Choose one person to serve as **moderator** to guide the discussion.

Also choose one **recorder** to take notes on important ideas to share with the full group.

MODERATOR: For each question, ask each person in your group to present and discuss ONE example or idea. If time permits, go back for more examples and discussions. Allow about 10 minutes for questions 1 and 2, and about 10 minutes for each segment of question 3. It is your responsibility to allow everyone to participate and to keep your group on time.

RECORDER: Please take notes on one _important_ example or idea from your group for each question. Others may take their own notes if they wish, but the recorder may be asked to summarize one successful practice for the full group at the end of the session.

I. SHARING SUCCESSFUL PRACTICES

What is _one_ of your school's successful practices to involve families in their children's education? Describe the practice, the grade levels involved, why you think this practice is important, **and what you or others in your school did to make the practice successful.**

PRACTICE? _____

_____

_____

_____

GRADE LEVELS? _____

_____

_____

_____

WHY IMPORTANT? _____

_____

_____

_____

WHAT MADE IT SUCCESSFUL?_____

_____

_____

_____

Use extra pages as needed.

152

2. JUMPING HURDLES

Describe one CHALLENGE or OBSTACLE that was overcome in order to successfully implement one practice to involve families at your school. What are some next steps that might make this practice even more effective?

PRACTICE? _____

_____

_____

_____

CHALLENGE? _____

_____

_____

_____

SOLUTION? _____

_____

_____

_____

NEXT STEPS? _____

_____

_____

_____

3. HARD-TO-REACH FAMILIES

In your school, which types of families are hardest to reach? Why are they hard to reach? What strategies and activities might improve your school's outreach and the families' involvement?

Hard-to-Reach Families	Main Reason	How Might We Involve These Families?
_____	_____	_____
_____	_____	_____
_____	_____	_____
_____	_____	_____
_____	_____	_____
_____	_____	_____
_____	_____	_____

153

4. LOOKING AHEAD: IMPROVING PRACTICES OF PARTNERSHIP

Here are a few goals and challenges for each type of involvement:

- Which practices might help your school with each type of involvement?
- How might these practices be designed *to reach all families in your school?*
- In your school, who might take leadership for these activities?

TYPE 1—PARENTING

Helping families understand each stage of their child's development
Practices: _____
Ways to reach all families: _____
Possible leaders at our school: _____

Getting information from workshops to all families who cannot attend
Practices: _____
Ways to reach all families: _____
Possible leaders at our school: _____

TYPE 2—COMMUNICATING

Helping families understand report cards
Practices: _____
Ways to reach all families: _____
Possible leaders at our school: _____

Setting conference schedules so all families can attend
Practices: _____
Ways to reach all families: _____
Possible leaders at our school: _____

Having newsletters that encourage two-way communication
Practices: _____
Ways to reach all families: _____
Possible leaders at our school: _____

TYPE 3—VOLUNTEERING

Recruiting and organizing volunteers to help students and the school
Practices: _____
Ways to reach all families: _____
Possible leaders at our school: _____

Scheduling events so that parents can attend as audiences
Practices: _____
Ways to reach all families: _____
Possible leaders at our school: _____

TYPE 4—LEARNING AT HOME

Providing families information on the skills required for students to pass each course

Practices: _____

Ways to reach all families: _____

Possible leaders at our school: _____

Designing and using interactive homework

Practices: _____

Ways to reach all families: _____

Possible leaders at our school: _____

TYPE 5—DECISION MAKING

Creating an active and helpful PTA/PTO

Practices: _____

Ways to reach all families: _____

Possible leaders at our school: _____

Enabling parents and teachers to work together on committees

Practices: _____

Ways to reach all families: _____

Possible leaders at our school: _____

Scheduling opportunities for the Action Team for School, Family, and Community Partnerships to report their work and progress to all teachers, parents, and others

Practices: _____

Ways to reach all families: _____

Possible leaders at our school: _____

TYPE 6—COLLABORATING WITH THE COMMUNITY

Identifying community resources to assist families, students, and school programs

Practices: _____

Ways to reach all families: _____

Possible leaders at our school: _____

Helping students, families, and educators contribute to their community

Practices: _____

Ways to reach all families: _____

Possible leaders at our school: _____

155

School Goals and
Results of Partnerships

This form helps the Action Team for School, Family, and Community Partnerships connect major school goals, desired results, and specific practices of partnership. Action Team members and others at school should discuss the following topics:

- *What major goals* have been set for students? These may be listed in your school improvement plan.

- *What measurable results must be produced* to reach your goals?

- *Which practices of school-family-community partnerships should be implemented or improved* to help produce the desired results for each goal?

Which specific changes in student attendance, attitudes, behavior, grades, or achievement test scores are needed? What are your statistics this year on attendance rates, disciplinary referrals, GPAs, reading, writing, math or other test scores, or other important indicators, and how do you want them to improve next year?

Which specific practices of partnership for all or some of the six types of involvement are most likely to help produce higher attendance (from the current rate), more positive attitudes (from an earlier measure), better math or writing skills (compared with last year's), or other results?

School Goals and Results of Partnerships

HOW MIGHT THE SIX TYPES OF INVOLVEMENT
HELP YOUR SCHOOL REACH ITS GOALS?

ONE ☆ MAJOR ☆ GOAL ☆ THAT OUR SCHOOL HAS SET IS: _____

_____

_____

_____

MEASURABLE RESULTS: How will you know when your school reaches THIS goal? (Specify the changes that you want to produce for the goal you listed above.) ____

_____

_____

_____

_____

PARTNERSHIP PRACTICES: Identify specific partnership activities that directly link to the goal. Then note the specific short-term results expected from each activity.

Some goals will be helped by practices in all six types of involvement; others may be helped by practices in just one or two types. Fill in activities only if they will help reach THIS goal.

Practices to help us reach THIS goal	Expected short-term results
Type 1—Parenting _____	_____
_____	_____
Type 2—Communicating _____	_____
_____	_____
Type 3—Volunteering _____	_____
_____	_____
Type 4—Learning at Home _____	_____
_____	_____
Type 5—Decision Making _____	_____
_____	_____
Type 6—Collaborating With the Community ____	_____
_____	_____

Linking Practices With Results

One of the greatest misconceptions about family involvement is that any practice increases student test scores. We have learned that the six types of involvement and various practices produce different, important results for students, families, and schools. This form encourages Action Teams to begin thinking about *specific results* that might be directly linked to practices for each of the six types of involvement. It also helps generate ideas about how the Action Team might realistically measure the expected results.

→ → Linking Practices With Results → →

For each type of involvement, identify *one* practice that would be useful to add or improve in your school. What *specific results* for students, families, or teachers do you expect from this practice? How might you measure whether the practice produces the results you expect?

TYPE 1—PARENTING → LINKS TO RESULTS

Practice: _____

_____

What *result(s)* **do you expect from** *this* **practice for students? families? teachers?**

_____

_____

How might you *measure* **the result(s) you listed?**

_____

_____

TYPE 2—COMMUNICATING → LINKS TO RESULTS

Practice: _____

_____

What *result(s)* **do you expect from** *this* **practice for students? families? teachers?**

_____

_____

How might you *measure* **the result(s) you listed?**

_____

_____

TYPE 3—VOLUNTEERING → LINKS TO RESULTS

Practice: _____

_____

What *result(s)* **do you expect from** *this* **practice for students? families? teachers?**

_____

_____

How might you *measure* **the result(s) you listed?**

_____

_____

TYPE 4—LEARNING AT HOME → LINKS TO RESULTS

Practice: _____

_____

What *result(s)* **do you expect from** *this* **practice for students? families? teachers?**

_____

_____

_____

How might you *measure* **the result(s) you listed?**

_____

_____

_____

TYPE 5—DECISION MAKING → LINKS TO RESULTS

Practice: _____

_____

What *result(s)* **do you expect from** *this* **practice for students? families? teachers?**

_____

_____

_____

How might you *measure* **the result(s) you listed?**

_____

_____

_____

TYPE 6—COLLABORATING WITH THE COMMUNITY → LINKS TO RESULTS

Practice: _____

_____

What *result(s)* **do you expect from** *this* **practice for students? families? teachers?**

_____

_____

_____

How might you *measure* **the result(s) you listed?**

_____

_____

_____

160

Summary of School Visits

When facilitators assist and visit more than one school, it is important to keep track of the work that gets done by the Action Team at each location. A visit may focus on a specific practice, the work of the Action Team, or other issues.

This form helps facilitators record information about the visits they make to assist Action Teams. It also should help facilitators conduct follow-up activities to assist each school's Action Team with its work. The Summary of School Visits should be completed *by the facilitator* after each visit.

Summary of School Visits

SCHOOL, FAMILY, AND COMMUNITY PARTNERSHIPS

Facilitator: _____

Date: _____ **Time of visit:** _____ **to** _____

School: _____

_____

Who initiated the visit? _____

_____

With whom did you meet? _____

_____

Focus and Content of Visit

What issues and/or challenges were discussed during the visit?

_____

_____

_____

_____

_____

_____

_____

What progress and/or decisions were made about the topics listed above?

_____

_____

_____

_____

_____

_____

_____

Facilitator notes—next steps and help needed:

_____

_____

_____

_____

_____

_____

Gathering Good Ideas

The Gathering Good Ideas form may be used or adapted to help educators and parents from many schools listen to and learn from each other. For example, an end-of-year workshop brings together the Action Teams from many schools to share information on the progress they made in improving partnerships during the year. They may present reports on best practices, discuss themes and issues on panels, describe problems and solutions, and exhibit best practices on tables or in booths. The Gathering Good Ideas form encourages attendees to take notes about activities that they might like to try in their schools.

Gathering Good Ideas

————

IDEAS TO STRENGTHEN ALL SIX TYPES OF INVOLVEMENT

What might you like to try in YOUR SCHOOL?
What questions do you have?
What information do you want?

TYPE 1: PARENTING—Assist families with parenting skills and setting home conditions to support children as students, and assist schools to understand families

Good Ideas

Questions?
What information do you need?

_____   _____

_____   _____

_____   _____

_____   _____

TYPE 2: COMMUNICATING—Conduct effective communications from school to home and from home to school about school programs and children's progress

Good Ideas

Questions?
What information do you need?

_____   _____

_____   _____

_____   _____

_____   _____

164

School, Family, and Community Partnerships by J. L. Epstein et al., © 1997 Corwin Press, Inc.
Photocopying permissible for local school use only.

TYPE 3: VOLUNTEERING—Organize volunteers and audiences to support the school and students

Good Ideas

Questions?
What information do you need?

_____   _____
_____   _____
_____   _____
_____   _____
_____   _____

TYPE 4: LEARNING AT HOME—Involve families with their children on homework and other curriculum-related activities and decisions

Good Ideas

Questions?
What information do you need?

_____   _____
_____   _____
_____   _____
_____   _____
_____   _____

TYPE 5: DECISION MAKING—Include families as participants in school decisions, and develop parent leaders and representatives

Good Ideas

Questions?
What information do you need?

_____   _____
_____   _____
_____   _____
_____   _____
_____   _____

TYPE 6: COLLABORATING WITH THE COMMUNITY—Coordinate resources and services from the community for families, students, and the school, and provide services to the community

Good Ideas

Questions?
What information do you need?

_____   _____
_____   _____
_____   _____
_____   _____
_____   _____

165

OTHER NOTES

_____
_____
_____
_____
_____
_____
_____
_____
_____
_____
_____
_____
_____
_____
_____
_____
_____
_____
_____
_____
_____
_____
_____
_____
_____
_____
_____
_____
_____
_____

Transitions: Involving Families When Students Move to New Schools

Transitions to new schools often confuse or concern children and parents. Research shows that family involvement drops dramatically when children move from elementary to middle school and from middle to high school. Families begin to lose touch with their children's school, and, as a result, they lose touch with their children as students.

To prevent this problem, elementary, middle, and high schools need to consider how they will prepare their students *and* families for transitions to new schools. For example, one high school designed a Type 2 Communications Project that included the following series of activities to help students and families move successfully from middle school to high school.

March	High school counselors and students meet during the school day with eighth-grade students *at the middle school.* **Families are invited.**
April	High school staff meet in the evening with eighth-grade students **and families** at the middle school. Information is provided to those who did not come.
May	Eighth-grade students visit the high school. **Families are invited.**
August	Ninth-grade students **and families** meet with teachers at the high school prior to the start of school. Information is provided to those who did not come.
September	Open house evening meeting is held for **all families** of students in Grades 9-12 at the high school. Information is provided to those who did not come.

The Type 2 Committee of the Action Team in this high school took the "challenge" to provide important information to all families of incoming ninth graders, including those who could not come to meetings held at the middle or high school. A similar plan could help children and families move from preschool to elementary school or from elementary to middle school.

On the accompanying charts, list the activities that your school could conduct to help students and their families make successful transitions *to your school* and from your school *to a new school.* Consider these points:

- How will you prepare *all* students and families for successful transitions to YOUR school or to a NEW school? What information do students and families need before the start of the school year? Which of your present activities will you continue or improve? What activities will you add to provide information, schedule visits, or conduct other activities?

- How might you work with educators in your "feeder" and "receiver" schools to develop, conduct, and evaluate your transitional activities?

You may revise the following charts to match your school year, account for more activities, or meet other needs of your students, families, and teachers.

Plan for Activities to Help Students and Families
Make Successful Transitions to *THIS* School

ACTIVITIES

January– Before Transition	
February	
March	
April	
May	
June	
July	
August	
September	
October	
Ongoing . . .	

What connections with your "feeder" schools would improve the activities you listed?

_____

_____

_____

School, Family, and Community Partnerships by J. L. Epstein et al., © 1997 Corwin Press, Inc.

Plan for Activities to Help Students and Families
Make Successful Transitions to *NEW* Schools

———————

ACTIVITIES

January– Before Transition	
February	
March	
April	
May	
June	
July	
August	
September	
October	
Ongoing . . .	

What connections with your "receiver" schools would improve the activities you listed?

_____

_____

_____

School, Family, and Community Partnerships by J. L. Epstein et al., © 1997 Corwin Press, Inc.

Sample Pledges
or Contracts

Pledges or contracts are symbolic agreements that formally recognize that students, families, teachers and administrators must work together to help students succeed each year in school. The form, content, and wording of pledges must be appropriate for preschool, elementary, middle, and high school levels, reflecting the developmental stages of the students, the organizational characteristics of the schools, and the situations of families as children move through the grades.

If you use pledges, we recommend that you create parallel forms for parents, students, teachers, and administrators. By signing parallel pledges, everyone becomes aware of their common goals, shared responsibilities, and personal commitments.

It helps to do the following:

- Use the term "pledge" instead of "contract" or "compact" to recognize the voluntary, good-faith nature of these commitments.

- Keep the list of commitments short and clear, including 5 to 10 items.

- Include a short cover letter signed by the principal that explains to students, families, and teachers that pledges are *part of* a comprehensive program of school, family, and community partnerships.

- Provide each teacher and family with signed copies.

- Implement school practices that enable parents, students, teachers and administrators to fulfill the commitments in the pledges. For example, if parents are asked to communicate with the school, then the school must provide clear information about how to contact teachers, counselors, or administrators. If parents are asked to volunteer, then the school must establish an effective program to recruit and welcome volunteers.

- Include an "open" item that students and families can insert to tailor the pledge to their own situations, interests, and needs.

- Discuss the content of pledges annually with students, families, teachers, and others; obtain input; and revise as needed.

- Develop a full program of partnerships including the six types of involvement. Pledges are one of many Type 2 communication strategies that strengthen school-family connections.

The sample pledges in this section should be tailored to match your school's policies and goals for students and for partnerships. Possible themes for parallel pledges are student effort, work, and behavior; attendance; communications from school to home and home to school such as conferences and meetings; volunteers; homework; study habits; appropriate dress; and specific school improvement goals.

SCHOOL-FAMILY-COMMUNITY PARTNERSHIPS
PARENT PLEDGE

✔   **I will help my child to do well in school. I will encourage my child to work hard in school and cooperate with teachers and other students.**

✔   **I will send my child to school on time each day with a positive attitude about school and about being a student. If my child is absent due to illness, I will see that the missed work is made up.**

✔   **I will read notices from the school and communicate with teachers or others about questions that I have about school programs or my child's progress. I will participate in parent-teacher-student conferences and other school events.**

✔   **I will check to see that my child completes the homework that is assigned. I will encourage my child to discuss homework, classwork, report card grades, and academic goals.**

✔   **I will volunteer to work at school <u>or</u> at home to conduct activities to assist my child, the teacher, class, and/or community. I will encourage my child to contribute talents and time to home, school, and community.**

SIGNATURE_____ DATE_____
                       Parent/Guardian

School, Family, and Community Partnerships by J. L. Epstein et al., © 1997 Corwin Press, Inc.

SCHOOL-FAMILY-COMMUNITY PARTNERSHIPS
STUDENT PLEDGE

✔ I will do my best in school. I will work hard and cooperate with my teachers and other students.

✔ I will attend school on time each day with a positive attitude about school and about being a student. If I am absent due to illness, I will make up classwork or homework that I missed.

✔ I will take notices home from school promptly and deliver notices to my teacher from home. I will participate in parent-teacher-student conferences, and inform my family about school activities and events.

✔ I will complete my homework assignments. I will discuss homework with my family to share what I am learning in class. I will discuss my report card grades and academic goals with my family.

✔ I will welcome volunteers to my school, and work with parents or others who assist me, my classmates, my teacher, or my school. I will contribute my talents and time to my family, school, and community.

SIGNATURE_____ DATE_____
Student

SCHOOL-FAMILY-COMMUNITY PARTNERSHIPS
TEACHER PLEDGE

✔ I will help all my students do their best in school. I will encourage each student to work hard, develop his or her talents, meet high expectations, and cooperate with teachers and students.

✔ I will come to school each day with a positive attitude about my students and their families, and with well-prepared classroom lessons to assist students' learning. I will help students and families understand and fulfill the school's attendance policies.

✔ I will communicate clearly and frequently so that all families understand school programs and their children's progress. I will enable families to contact me with questions about their children. I will conduct at least one parent-teacher-student conference with each family.

✔ I will use interactive homework that enables students to discuss and demonstrate skills at home that we are learning in class. I will guide families to monitor their children's homework and to discuss report card grades and academic goals with their children.

✔ I will arrange ways for parents or other volunteers to use their time and talents to assist my students at school, in my class, or at home. I will vary schedules to encourage families to attend events, assemblies, and celebrations at school.

SIGNATURE_____ DATE_____
Teacher

SCHOOL-FAMILY-COMMUNITY PARTNERSHIPS
ADMINISTRATOR PLEDGE

✔ I will encourage all students to do their best in school. I will encourage each student to work hard, develop his or her talents, meet high expectations, and cooperate with teachers, the school staff, and other students.

✔ I will come to school each day with a positive attitude about my faculty, students, and their families and communities. I also will help my faculty, families, and students understand, contribute to, and fulfill the school's attendance and other policies.

✔ I will communicate clearly and frequently so that all families understand the school's programs and their children's progress. I will encourage families to contact teachers and administrators with questions and ideas about their children and about school programs. I also will support and assist teachers to conduct at least one parent-teacher-student conference with each family each year.

✔ I will assist teachers, families, and students to understand and discuss homework policies, report card grades, academic goals, and support other activities that encourage family involvement in student learning.

✔ I will arrange ways for parents or other volunteers to use their time and talents to assist students and the school. I also will encourage families to attend events, assemblies, and celebrations at school.

✔ I will help develop a comprehensive program of school, family, and community partnerships at this school.

SIGNATURE_____ DATE_____
                    Administrator

7

More Information on Middle and High Schools, Homework, and Surveys

This chapter contains the following additional information and resources for developing strong programs of school-family-community partnerships:

- Reports on Partnerships in the Middle Grades and High Schools

- Teachers Involve Parents in Schoolwork (TIPS) Processes. Descriptions of TIPS interactive homework for the elementary and middle grades and TIPS social studies and art volunteers for the middle grades

- Surveys and Summaries: Questionnaires on School and Family Partnerships. Information about surveys for teachers and parents in the elementary and middle grades and for teachers, parents, and students in high schools

Reports on Partnerships in the Middle Grades and High Schools

This section includes summaries to assist *middle schools* and *high schools* in developing comprehensive programs of school, family, and community partnerships.

Middle Schools

"School and Family Partnerships" is a reprint of a 1992 special issue of *The Practitioner,* published by the National Association of Secondary School Principals, and discusses the six types of involvement in the middle grades.

For more information, see "School and Family Partnerships in the Middle Grades" by Joyce L. Epstein and Lori J. Connors, in *Creating Family/School Partnerships,* edited by B. Rutherford (Columbus, OH: National Middle School Association, 1995), pp. 137-165; and "Improving School-Family-Community Partnerships in the Middle Grades," by Joyce L. Epstein, in *Middle School Journal,* November 1996, pp. 43-48. These articles link partnerships to other recommendations for middle-level school improvement.

High Schools

"High Schools Gear Up to Create Effective School and Family Partnerships," pp. 1-4 in *Research and Development Report,* No. 5, Center on Families, Communities, Schools and Children's Learning, June 1994, is a summary of two reports on the six types of involvement in high schools.

For more information, see the March 1995 special issue of *The High School Magazine* on parent involvement.

School and Family Partnerships in Middle Grades and High Schools*

Joyce L. Epstein and Lori J. Connors

Most parents love their children and want the best for them, but many do not know how to translate their care and concern into positive involvement in education. Families need more information and guidance from the schools to enable them to maintain an ongoing dialogue with their adolescents about school, growing up, and their future. The nature and content of school-family partnerships change through the years, along with adolescents, their families, and their schools.

- *Students are changing.* Adolescent needs and ideas about themselves differ from those of younger children. They need opportunities to develop their independence and take more responsibility for themselves, even as they continue to need adults to guide and support them. Adolescents must balance peer relationships with adult relationships as they seek the comfort of conformity with their peers and pursue the identification of their uniqueness as individuals.

- *Families are changing.* The family unit is changing. Parents may be older, mothers may work full-time or part-time, families may be headed by a single parent, and families may live further away from the school. Parents may be confused about their adolescents' development and worried about the problems that face adolescents in the 1990s. Middle-level and high schools must design and organize family involvement to meet parents' needs and fit the realities of family life. They must help youngsters build independence while helping parents become knowledgeable partners with the schools.

- *Schools are changing.* Middle-level and high schools are organized and staffed differently from most elementary schools. They are usually larger, fully departmentalized, and have more teachers certified for the secondary grades, educated as subject matter experts, and unprepared to work with families. School and family partnerships must be organized to make the best use of the various adults who have important roles in middle and high schools. Even with these changes, the concept of partnership persists across the grades. In the middle-level and high school grades, partnerships are, in fact, three-way—family-student-school—because of the increasing maturity of adolescents and their changing relationships with adults.

---

* The first half of this section is reprinted from an article in *NASSP Practitioner, 18*(4), June 1992. The second half is adapted from that article.

Family Environment and Involvement

Parental encouragement, support, appropriate supervision and guidance, and positive communications about school and learning positively influence student achievement, grades, attitudes, aspirations, and behavior. Although, on average, more highly educated families are more involved, families from all situations—regardless of the formal education or income level of the parents, and regardless of the grade level or ability of the student—use strategies to encourage and influence their children's education. Studies show that parents' involvement in education can help compensate for the lack of other family resources and help more youngsters define themselves as students. The benefits accrue for all students, including those from families with less education or fewer economic advantages.

The early studies documenting the importance of family environments for student success opened a new research question: *If* family involvement and encouragement is important, *how* can we help more families at all grade levels become involved in ways that help their children succeed in school?

This question guides the development and evaluation of school partnership programs with families. Research is accumulating that shows schools must take a leadership role to enable more parents to become and remain involved in their children's education. When schools take these steps, more families appreciate the assistance and become successful partners, and more students benefit in achievements, attitudes, and behaviors. As they develop school and family partnerships, educators should consider the following:

- Families remain important to adolescents, even as peers become more important.

- School-family partnership practices are declining dramatically at each grade level. Coincidentally, with each year in school, more families report that they are unable to assist their children and understand the schools. Schools correct this when they implement comprehensive partnership programs.

- Most parents cannot and do not participate at the school building level, either as volunteers or in decision-making and leadership roles.

- By contrast, most parents, including up to 90% at the middle level and 80% in high schools, want to know how to help their own children at home, and what to do to help them succeed at school. Studies of middle-level and high schools, and of public, Catholic, and other private schools confirm that families need and want more information and guidance from the schools.

- The social, academic, and personal problems that increase in adolescence require the concerted attention of all who share an interest and investment in children. The efforts of schools and families have not been well-organized to date. Each institution usually works separately, often without knowledge of or communication with the others.

The community also has a contribution to make, but community services and resources often have been applied without collaboration or communication with schools or families.

This disorganized delivery of services has contributed to the failure of many students to reach their potential. It helps explain the well-known and unacceptable statistics on school failure, retentions in grade, drug and alcohol abuse, delinquency, teen pregnancy, and the other problems that increase in adolescence.

Involving families will not by itself make students successful learners or high achievers. That takes the hard work of teachers, administrators, and the students themselves on a daily agenda of excellence. Nevertheless, even in good schools, more students will benefit, go farther, and reach higher if they are part of successful school, family, and community partnerships extending through the secondary school years.

Developing Comprehensive Programs of Partnership

A research-based framework of six major types of involvement has been devised to help educators develop more comprehensive programs of school-family partnerships. Each type of involvement includes different practices that are likely to lead to *different outcomes* for students, parents, teaching practice, and school climate. Here, we outline the major types of involvement and provide a few general examples and others that may be important for accommodating particular adolescents, families, and schools.

TYPE 1: BASIC OBLIGATIONS OF FAMILIES

Schools must provide families with information about adolescent health and safety, supervision, nutrition, discipline and guidance, parenting skills, and parenting approaches. This information helps families build positive home environments that support learning through high school. Some schools offer parent workshops and other forms of parent education, training, and information sharing.

Families continue to teach their children attitudes, beliefs, customs, behaviors, and skills that, apart from the school curriculum, are unique to and valued by the family. Schools are enriched by the varying backgrounds and cultures of the students' families. This two-way exchange—information to help families understand child and adolescent development and information to help schools understand family life and students' needs, interests, and talents—is at the heart of Type 1 activities, which may include helping families understand early and late adolescence, supporting adolescent health and mental health, and preventing key problems in adolescent development.

Families may want information (and may want to give the school information) about how to meet adolescents' simultaneous needs for increased independence and continued guidance; about understanding the importance of peers and the risks of peer pressure; and about other topics. Families may want to know more about setting appropriate family rules, providing decision-making opportunities to adolescents, and changing discipline practices to support student development. With appropriate information, families can establish home conditions that help students balance studying, homework, part-time jobs, and home chores.

The challenge of successful Type 1 activities is to provide information to all families who want it and need it, not just the few who can attend workshops at the school. This information can be provided by videos, tape recordings, handouts, newsletters and cable broadcasts, for example.

TYPE 2: BASIC OBLIGATIONS OF SCHOOLS

This category refers to the communications from schools to families about school programs and students' progress. It includes the usual notices, memos, phone calls, report cards, conferences, open-house nights or other opportunities that most schools conduct, and other more innovative communications.

It may include information to help families to choose or change schools, if the district has such a policy. Schools must vary the form and frequency of communications so the information sent home can be understood by all families.

Type 2 communications help families help students select curricula, courses, special programs, and other activities each year. Information about report card grading systems helps families monitor student progress in school and helps families help students improve their grades. Parent-teacher conferences allow parents and students to meet with teachers of all subjects in efficient, productive, and friendly meetings.

Families need information at important transitions from elementary to middle level and from middle level to high school. Orientation sessions at these points recognize that families make transitions with their children and, if informed, can help students adjust to new schools.

At other key points in schooling, families need information to help students plan for college and work; to begin financial savings for education and training; to learn about scholarships, loans, and grants; and to plan for college and jobs.

The challenge of Type 2 activities is to make communications clear and understandable for all families so they can respond wisely; to incorporate two-way systems so families can initiate and respond to communications; and to help students become partners by taking information home and by discussing schoolwork and school-related decisions with their families.

TYPE 3: INVOLVEMENT AT SCHOOL

Parents and others need to volunteer at the school or in classrooms, and families should come to school for student performances, sports, or other events. Schools increase the number of families who come to the school building by varying schedules so that more can participate as volunteers or serve as audiences at different times of the day and evening.

Volunteers can be put to better use in middle-level and high schools if a coordinator matches volunteers' times and skills with the needs of teachers, administrators, and students. Programs that tap parents' talents, occupations, and interests can enrich subject classes and improve career explorations.

Mentoring, coaching, and tutoring activities may be particularly helpful as students' skills, interests, and talents become increasingly diverse in the upper grades.

The challenge of Type 3 activities is to recruit volunteers widely, make hours flexible for parents who work during the school day, and enable volunteers to contribute productively to the school and the curriculum. A real challenge is to change the definition of "volunteer" to mean any one, any time, any place who supports school goals or student learning. This opens up possibilities for more parents and other community members to be volunteers. A special challenge for middle-level and high schools is to encourage students to volunteer service to their school, to assist other students who need help, and to provide and recognize the services they perform for their families and communities.

Type 3 activities help increase families' comfort and familiarity with the school and staff, students' communications with adults, and teachers' awareness of parents' willingness to contribute substantively to the school and to communicate with other parents.

TYPE 4: INVOLVEMENT IN HOME LEARNING

Teachers must guide parents in monitoring, assisting, and interacting with their own children at home on learning activities that are coordinated with classwork or that contribute to success in school. This involvement also includes parent-initiated, student-initiated, and teacher-directed discussions about homework or school subjects.

Schools help families become more knowledgeable about curriculum by providing information about academic and other skills required to pass each grade; methods to monitor, discuss, and help with homework; and ways to help students practice and study for tests.

It must be clear that the school does not expect families to "teach" school subjects but to encourage, listen, react, praise, guide, monitor, and discuss the work the students bring home. This may be done by interactive homework, student-teacher-family "contracts," long-term projects, or other interactive strategies that encourage students and families to talk about schoolwork at home. Families must interact with students in ways that help them become more independent learners.

The challenge of Type 4 activities is to design a regular schedule of interactive work that enables students to discuss the important and interesting things they are learning, interview family members, record reactions, and share written work.

Students learn that the school wants their families to know what they are learning and to talk over ideas and school decisions at home. A weekly or biweekly schedule keeps families aware of the depth of the curriculum and their children's progress.

TYPE 5: INVOLVEMENT IN DECISION MAKING, GOVERNANCE, AND ADVOCACY

Parents and others in the community should hold participatory roles in parent-teacher-student organizations, school advisory councils, school site improvement teams, Title I, and other school committees. This type of involvement sees parents as activists in community educational advocacy groups.

Schools strengthen parent participation in school decisions by encouraging the organization of parent groups and committees and by training parents and students in leadership and decision-making skills. Schools can assist advocacy groups by providing information to bolster community support for school improvement. Committees' involvement is important in curriculum, safety, supplies and equipment, career development, and school improvement.

A special challenge of Type 5 activities is to include parent leaders from all racial and ethnic groups, socioeconomic levels, and geographic communities in the school. An even more difficult challenge is helping parent-leaders act as true representatives of other families, with good two-way communication. A third challenge is including students in decision-making groups and leadership positions.

TYPE 6: COLLABORATION AND EXCHANGES WITH THE COMMUNITY

Schools, families, and students must establish connections with agencies, businesses, cultural groups, and community organizations that share responsibility for young people's education and their future successes. This activity includes school coordination of student access to community and support services, such as after-school recreation, tutorial programs, health services, and cultural events.

Schools draw on community resources to provide parent education in adolescent development (Type 1), improve schools' communications with families (Type 2), increase the number of community volunteers at the school or to enlist business support for parent-workers to volunteer or attend activities at the school (Type 3), enhance the curriculum and other experiences of students (Type 4), and extend participation on school committees to business and community representatives (Type 5).

The challenge of Type 6 activities is to solve the problems usually associated with community-school connections—for example, poor communications about the mission, strengths, and needs of the school, "turf" problems of who decides what community resources are needed or how they will be allocated and supervised, and other difficulties that lead to fragmented and selective distribution of services. Type 6 activities increase the knowledge of families, students, and schools about the resources they can tap in their community.

What Should Educators Do With This Framework?

Each school must decide which practices it needs to develop a comprehensive program of school and family connections. Teachers, parents, administrators, and students must know where they are starting from and how they would like their programs and practices to grow over time.

The following questions may help principals and their school and family partnership teams organize their work:

- Which partnership practices are currently working well at each grade level? What are the starting points for each of the major types of involvement?

- Which partnership practices should be improved or added in each grade?

- How do you want the school's family involvement practices to look three years from now? Which present practices should continue and which should change? What new practices are needed for each of the major types of involvement to reach school goals?

- Are the practices of school and family partnership coherent and coordinated or fragmented? Are families separated by categories (e.g., Title I, limited English proficient, special education) or brought together as a school community?

- Which families are you reaching and which families are "hard to reach"? What can be done to communicate better with these families?

- What do teachers expect of families? What do families expect of teachers and others at school? What do students expect their families to do to help them negotiate school life? How do students help their teachers keep their families informed and involved?

- How are students succeeding on important measures of achievement, attitude, attendance, and other indicators of success? How could families assist the school to help more students reach higher goals and greater success?

- Who will be responsible for developing and implementing partnership practices? Will staff development be needed? How will teachers, administrators, parents, and students be supported and recognized for their work?

- What costs are associated with the improvements you want? Will small grants or other special funding be needed?

- How will you evaluate the implementation and results of your efforts? How will you know whether and how well the goals you set have been accomplished? What indicators, observations, and other measures will be used?

- How will you ensure that program development continues to improve practices and to increase the number of families who are partners with the school? What opportunities will you arrange for teachers, parents, and students to share information on successful practices in order to strengthen their own efforts?

As with other school improvement processes, it helps to have a written policy to identify goals and a plan of action. A leadership and a committee structure must be established to accept responsibility for the conduct and progress of the plan. There must be a budget for program development; time to think, work, and share ideas; and evaluation of the implementation processes and results.

Developing notable partnerships takes three to five years. During this time, schools improve their capabilities to work with families; more families become involved in their children's education; and more students benefit from their families' knowledge, interest, and encouragement.

To Illustrate . . .

There are hundreds of different practices that help schools develop each type of involvement. Some evaluations of practices have been conducted in the middle grades and high schools, but more are needed. Research over the next few years should improve what we know about the effects of specific practices in the middle and high school grades so that schools can select practices more purposefully. Here are a few examples of how some middle and high schools put the major types of involvement into practice.

Type 1—Helping families with basic parenting of adolescents and building home conditions that support the work of middle and high school students

- In New York City, a **series of workshops** was developed for parents of adolescents which focused on effective communication, adolescent development, handling stress, preparing youngsters for college, and understanding school policies and procedures. The challenge in this kind of activity, as noted above, is to find ways to provide the information from the workshop to those who were unable to come but who need and want the information.

- In St. Paul, Minnesota, the schools and area businesses established a downtown **Working Parent Resource Center**. The center provides working parents with books, videos, classes, and other resources from infancy through the high school grades.

- In other districts, parent centers were established in the community. More schools are creating family rooms or parent clubs in their school buildings to have a place for parents to exchange information, hold workshops and classes for families and students, and encourage other contacts of families and school staffs.

- In Albuquerque, New Mexico, Chapter 1 funds were used to hire a **Home-School Liaison** in one middle school and one high school. The liaison contacted families by phone and made home visits to help students improve attendance and achievement. Other home-school coordinators in middle and high schools in Anchorage, Alaska and in Seattle, Washington helped families understand and improve their supervision of their children as students and their home support for learning. Paid professional staff are important for sustained, successful programs, particularly to assist the families of students who are at risk of failing or who face serious problems in adolescence.

- Other Type 1 practices in middle and high schools include courses for parents in adult education, GED, and English language; workshops for parents on difficult topics to discuss at home such as teen sexuality and drug abuse; workshops attended by parents and teens; sessions for parents to talk with each other; and activities to help teachers meet and understand the families of their students.

Type 2—Communicating with families in understandable terms and useful forms about school programs and students' progress

- In a Baltimore City middle school, new sixth-grade students and their families attended **Orientation Days** on the first days of school. Activities involved families and students together for a day at the school—meeting teachers, receiving information about the school program, and experiencing classes together. Evaluations indicated high participation by families and positive reactions of students, parents, and middle grades teachers.

- **Newsletters** were improved at another Baltimore middle school to keep families informed of school programs and also to summarize workshops that most families could not attend.

- Newsletters at a high school were mailed to families and included timely information on high school students' courses, graduation requirements, and other programs.

- In Indianapolis, parent-teacher conferences and frequent communications were major initiatives of the **Parents in Touch** program. In middle and high schools, conferences were scheduled so that working parents could attend; folders included policies, graduation requirements, and students' course records; "contracts" were signed by parents, students, and teachers; and a computerized phone information system was installed. A number of school systems have begun to use **telephone answering machines, electronic mailboxes, or computerized phone message systems** to give parents daily or weekly information about homework assignments, class activities, notices about meetings or upcoming deadlines, and ideas of how to help students at home.

- Some communications seek to ease the transition from elementary to middle, from middle to high school, and from high school to work or college. For example, a middle grades administrator in Michigan called parents of all new students after one week to make personal contact with the families and to check on parents' perceptions of students' adjustment.

- Other Type 2 practices include giving families advance notice about special schedules, costs, and other requirements; conferences at home with parents who have no transportation to get to the school; helping parents of students at risk of failing to monitor homework and schoolwork to encourage students to raise report card grades; and other communications.

Type 3—Volunteers and audiences at school to strengthen school goals and programs, and in all locations to assist and support students

- The Teachers Involve Parents In Schoolwork (TIPS) Social Studies and Art process established a **teacher-volunteer partnership** where parents or other volunteers introduce artists to students in 20-minute class presentations designed to integrate art with the social studies curriculum in the middle grades. In one Baltimore middle school, a teacher coordinator and a parent coordinator worked together to select and order art prints linked to social studies, plan presentations, and train volunteers. Evaluations showed that students increased their knowledge and appreciation of art and that parents and other volunteers can be involved productively in the middle grades.

- In a Minnesota high school, **parent volunteers** helped students research careers, locate college and vocational information, and coordinate college visits at a career center.

- Other volunteer activities in middle and high schools included making cassette tapes for students to read along when their science or social studies books are at a reading level beyond their own reading skills.

Type 4—Involving families in students' learning activities at home, including interactive homework, discussions of school subjects, and keeping schoolwork on the agenda at home

- In Illinois, two sets of **videotapes** for junior high parents were produced in cooperation with the local cable company. The parent education tapes showed parents effective ways to motivate their children to learn. "Critical lessons" were tapes of class sessions in different subjects that students and families could discuss at home to share the content of schoolwork.

- **Summer Home Learning Packets** were designed to provide middle grades students in Baltimore City with opportunities to practice skills and continue learning over the summer with encouragement and involvement from their families. Packets were mailed home during the summer. Evaluations showed that students who worked with parents completed more summer assignments, and that some students, particularly those with marginal skills to start, who completed more did better than expected on skills in the fall.

- **Teachers Involve Parents in Schoolwork (TIPS) Interactive Homework** activities for middle grades language arts and science/health were developed with teachers to design homework that required students to talk to a parent or other family member in order to complete the assignment. Evaluations showed that TIPS homework can be implemented successfully in the middle grades, that families greatly appreciated the interactions with their early adolescents, and that students learned some things about their families that they would not otherwise have known.

- Other examples of Type 4 activities included a middle grades math program in Ohio that had specially designed demonstration forms for students to share each newly mastered math skill with their families to document and celebrate progress. The curricular materials to discuss at home were produced by teachers and district curriculum supervisors.

Type 5—Involving families in school decision making and advocacy

- In Dallas, a parent/public relations organization raised and distributed funds to the 25 high schools and magnet schools in the city. Each high school's parent group designed message boards, brochures, newsletters, or arranged events to highlight school accomplishments based on the needs of the school community.

- School-site management teams, advisory councils, and committees are other Type 5 activities that are becoming more common in middle and high schools.

Type 6—Collaborations and exchanges with the community

- A program of the National Association of State Boards of Education (NASBE) awarded grants to assist communities in promoting positive family relationships, particularly parent-adolescent communications.

- In Ohio, **Parent Educational Parties** were conducted in the homes of middle and high school students to promote better coordination of community services, family needs, and student success in school. The informational, educational parties for families of students enrolled in the program concentrated on increasing parental involvement in their teens' education and empowering parents with advocacy skills.

- In Minnesota, the legislature enacted a **state law** that requires employers to allow employees who are parents to take up to 16 hours of time to be involved in their children's education through high school. This includes attending conferences with their children's teachers and other activities at the schools. The state of Virginia passed similar legislation applying to state employees to serve as a model for other employers to recognize the importance of family support for their children's schools. This community connection links businesses and government with families and schools.

- A **School-Based Youth Services Program** in New Jersey coordinates education, health, and recreation services for 13- to 19-year-olds at 29 sites at or near high schools and some middle schools. The program has solved many of the problems associated with integrated services programs.

- Many schools have business partnerships for improving school programs, students' career explorations and opportunities, and teacher internships. Other Type 6 activities include school-sponsored telephone referral systems to community services for teens and families; work-site seminars for workshops for parents who cannot come to the school; and other community partnerships that help schools, students, and families.

COMPREHENSIVE SCHOOL AND FAMILY PARTNERSHIPS

As schools work from year to year to add and improve practices of partnership with families and the community, their programs become more comprehensive, covering all six types of involvement. Examples of comprehensive efforts are the following:

- In Texas, a program created for immigrant students served families of middle and high school students new to the United States. The program incorporated all of the major types of involvement, including workshops and classes in parent education and family English language skills development, communications from the school to the home in Spanish, volunteers at school, guided parent-child interactions on schoolwork at home—particularly writing and language arts activities, parents on advisory councils in decision-making roles, and community connections about school through the use of the families' favorite radio and TV stations and local newspaper. Parent coordinators and community aides helped the schools coordinate activities; community partners provided resources to support school programs, and, in partnership with the local radio station, produced a weekly program in Spanish that encouraged families to become more involved in their children's education. Working with families who many other schools find "hard to reach," this program illustrated the reach-ability of all families when programs are based on the concept of partnership.

- In Boston, a middle school implemented practices of all six types of involvement, including workshops, home visits, and a parent room or office; communications in print, phone, and other forms; volunteers; learning activities at home including a read-aloud program; parents in decision-making roles including a representative for each homeroom to keep all parents informed via telephone trees and other networks; and business, university, community, and school partnerships.

- In California, a statewide policy on parent involvement and policies in many districts, set guidelines for schools to encourage the development of comprehensive programs of all six types of involvement. To help its schools implement its state and district policies, San Diego County developed a resource book containing sample practices for many types of involvement. The county also installed a computerized telephone information system and produced a monthly television show, *Parent Hour,* to provide information to parents and opportunities for them to raise questions. Many schools in California continue to work toward comprehensive programs that reach more families.

Endnote

Middle and high schools have tended to lag behind preschools and elementary schools in developing comprehensive programs to involve families. In most middle and high school improvement plans, parent involvement is on the list of needed components but is often left aside or treated casually. Now, with the heightened awareness of the importance of the shared responsibilities of schools and families in the education and development of adolescents, and with advances in theories, research, policies, and practices of partnership, the time is right for middle and high school leaders to join the agenda.

High Schools Gear Up to Create
Effective School and Family Partnerships[1]

Parent involvement in their children's schooling declines dramatically as students move from the elementary grades through middle school and high school. But students continue to want and need the support of their parents and other adults to help them reach their educational goals.

Center researchers Joyce L. Epstein and Lori J. Connors have been working with six high schools—two urban, two suburban, and two rural—in a collaborative effort to identify what parent-school partnership practices are appropriate at the high school level, how the schools can develop and implement such practices, and how the practices actually affect the students, parents, and teachers involved.

In a series of meetings, Epstein and Connors and teams from each school discussed the schools' current practices–what they were already doing to involve families and their ideas for doing more. Each school also administered surveys to ninth-grade teachers, parents, and students to provide information from each group about attitudes and beliefs about family involvement and the school, current practices considered weak or strong, levels of current parent involvement (including school practices for reaching out to contact parents), and demographic and school-specific information. The researchers have analyzed the data provided by these surveys and summarized the preliminary results, which are being used by the schools to develop multiyear action plans for a comprehensive and responsive set of family partnership practices at the high school level.

Current Practices and Ideas: Some Blue-Chip Stocks in the Trust Fund, But Some Junk Bonds Too

The six high schools are all part of Maryland's Tomorrow—a state drop-out prevention initiative that puts family involvement on the school agenda. These high schools thus already had some practices underway, although none had worked systematically to develop a program. Epstein and Connors describe where these schools are starting from—the existing practices in each school—as a "trust fund," recognizing that each school's past practices can be built upon to create further partnerships and also recognizing that trust is a primary element in the effort to develop comprehensive practices of partnership over time.[2]

An action team from each school and Center researchers Epstein and Connors collaborated to identify their trust funds—a combination of existing practices and ideas for further practices. The schools and researchers categorized the activities that were being conducted according to the six-type framework developed by Epstein to help schools build strong family, school, and community partnerships.

Type 1: Parenting/Adolescent Development. This refers to schools helping to improve parents' understanding of adolescent development, parenting skills, and the conditions at home for learning. The school also seeks to improve its own understanding of the families of its students. Activities and ideas in the trust funds of the six high schools included home visits, family support groups, referrals for special services, social services, providing information to parents about teens, and providing parenting skills for teen parents.

Type 2: Communicating. This refers to the basic obligation of schools to improve the communications from school to home and from home to school about school programs and students' progress through the use of letters, memos, report cards, newsletters, conferences, and other mechanisms. Activities and ideas included easing the transition to high school (orientation letters, tours for middle-grade students, summer and fall orientations for students and parents), holding back-to-school nights, signing pledges/contracts with parents, using phone and mail communications (including newsletters), holding conferences, and providing information on school policies and programs.

Type 3: Volunteering. This refers to the involvement in school of parent and community volunteers, and the involvement of parents and others who come to the school to support and watch student performances, sports, and other events. High school practices and ideas included volunteer activities (parents help other parents, call about attendance, talk about their careers, mentor students) and increasing family attendance at school events.

Type 4: Learning Activities at Home. This refers to improving family involvement in learning activities at home, including involvement in homework, classwork, and curricular-related interactions and decisions. Activities and ideas from the high schools included helping parents to help students set goals and select courses, providing college information, and conducting career transition programs.

Type 5: Decision Making. This refers to parents and other community residents in advisory, decision-making, or advocacy roles in parent associations, advisory committees, and school improvement or school-site councils. It also refers to parent and community activists in independent advocacy groups that work for school improvement. The six high schools' activities and ideas included creating more active parent organizations and increasing the numbers of parents, students, and community members in advisory and decision-making groups.

Type 6: Collaborating With the Community. This refers to activities of schools, families, or students involving any of the community organizations or institutions that share some responsibility for children's development and success. High school activities and ideas included community involvement in school-linked health care programs, delineating a clear role for families in business-school partnerships, offering workshops at school about community resources, and informing families about students' community service activities and requirements.

Thus the high schools, with their current practices and their ideas for more, had trust funds upon which to build. Some were better endowed than others, and some of the endowments were more idea based than practice based.

Epstein and Connors (1994) note that

> in these high schools, as in most others, past efforts of partnership have been limited. Few parents are informed about or involved in their teens' education. Even the most basic communications are not systematized to reach all families, and many are limited to negative messages or discussions about students' problems. Families are rarely guided to conduct discussions with their teens about important school decisions or plans for their future.

The next task was to examine the schools' current practices and ideas, make improvements, and add other practices based on the specific needs of their school's teachers, students, and families. These needs were identified through surveys conducted by each school, with the data for each analyzed by the researchers on the project.

Survey Results: Teachers, Students, and Parents Provide Information for Building Partnerships

Teachers, students, and parents, through the surveys, discussed their attitudes toward their school and the importance of family involvement and contributed their thoughts about the current condition of parent involvement practices at the high school, what practices they would like to see put into place, and suggestions for next steps that should be taken.

Four themes emerged from Connors and Epstein's (1994) analyses of the data on attitudes: school and community relationships, importance of parent involvement and willingness to be involved, time and training for school-family partnership activities, and the frequency, amount, and type of homework assigned.[3]

There is much agreement by all three groups of respondents in these areas, with some differences. Teachers, parents, and students at all six high schools worry about their communities being unsafe and not having good after-school and evening activities for teens—in general, recognizing that all the schools need to strengthen connections with their communities. At the same time, they tend to rate their school itself as a good place (78% of parents, 62% of students, and 49% of teachers), and more than 90% of parents reported being welcome at their teen's high school.

More than 90% of the parents and teachers and 82% of the students agreed that parent involvement was needed at the high school level. And many parents (more than 80%) said they wanted to be more involved, a view supported by more than 50% of students, who want their parents to be more involved. Only 32% of the teachers, however, felt that it was their responsibility to involve parents.

Further agreement among teachers, students, and parents occurs on the issue of time—no one has a lot to spare. About 50% of the teachers say they don't have enough time to involve families; about 50% of students say they don't have enough time to talk to their parents about school or homework, and about 25% of parents say they do not have enough time to talk with their teens on a daily basis about school.

School Practices. Teachers, parents, and students rated how well their school was conducting activities within the six types of school-family-community partnership practices. They identified practices that were currently strong, needed improvement, or needed to be added, forming a profile of "opportunities for growth" for each school. Again, there were many areas of agreement among the groups but also some differences.

In all the high schools, parents (72%), students (61%), and teachers (95%) believed that the school should start or improve practices to help parents understand more about adolescent development. Teachers, parents, and students also felt that communication practices should be improved in three ways: reach more families with information about school programs and student progress; contact families more often with positive news about students; and provide more information to help students plan their futures. Teachers (88%) clearly supported the idea that more parents and other community members should volunteer to help at school—but 70% of the parents noted that they had never been asked to volunteer. Students weren't entirely sold on the idea of their parents being active in the school—40% thought it was not important to "invite my parents to become volunteers," 22% said it was not important to "invite parents to school programs or events," and 55% said "No, don't ask my parent to go on a class trip."

Teachers, parents, and students in all six schools "felt that practices to assist parents in monitoring and improving student homework should be developed or strengthened," Connors and Epstein note. At the same time, most parents say they are doing the four practices that teachers think are most important: checking homework (85% of parents say they talk to their teens about homework); talking to their teens about school at home (94% of parents say they do this); telling their teens that school is important (88% of parents say they do this), and helping their teens balance activities (88% of parents say they help their teens plan time for homework, chores, and other responsibilities).

All groups agreed that parents should be included (a) on committees to review school policy and the curriculum and (b) in other decision-making groups. Many students (70%) said that they too want to be included on committees that make decisions about the school. As for community involvement—parents and students say that the best thing communities can do is provide employment or job training to teens. More than 80% of the parents wanted information on summer and part-time jobs for teens; more than 70% wanted information on job training for teens; and the students themselves wanted information about job training (56%) and after-school jobs (65%).

"The activities that parents, students, and teachers would like their school to begin or improve were similar for schools in city, suburban, and rural locations," Connors and Epstein (1994) note. "High school teachers, students, and families have a surprisingly common vision of high schools that inform and involve families in their teens' education."

Themes and Issues in Developing High School Partnerships With Families and Communities

Several general themes and issues have emerged from the collaborative effort of the researchers and high schools to create school-family-community partnerships that have implications for the design of programs and their progress. For example:

Barriers Exist That Hinder Development. The school action teams identified 10 barriers to effective school and family partnerships in high schools. A partial list includes teachers' assumptions that many parents are uninterested in their children's education, teachers' lack of knowledge about effective practices or how to adapt practices, and families' transportation, child care, and work schedule problems.

Home-to-School Information Is Needed. Schools need but don't get enough of the good information that families can provide about their teenagers' talents and needs.

The Mail Doesn't Always Get Through. Schools have little confidence that students will carry messages and reports home to their families, but mailing is not much better—it takes money, address lists are difficult to keep up to date, and many students intercept the mail from the school before a parent can get it.

Students Must Be in the Loop. At the high school level, students must be active participants in school-family-community partnerships.

Some Practices Are More Pertinent for High Schools. A number of basic practices for each of the six types of school-family-community partnerships are especially appropriate in high schools. To improve parenting skills, schools can provide useful and easy-to-read information about adolescent development; to improve communications, schools should establish strong connections with parents at the point of transition between middle grades and high schools; to organize volunteers effectively, schools should recruit and coordinate volunteers to help students explore occupations and work sites; to involve families in learning at home, schools should provide materials and information about setting academic goals, making college choices, and carrying out post-secondary plans.

Understanding Partnerships in High Schools

There are reasons why parent involvement drops off drastically in high schools. And each of these reasons becomes a special topic that programs of school-family-community partnerships at the high school level have to deal with. These include the needs that adolescents have for more autonomy and responsibility, more working parents who live further from the high schools, the more complex organization of the high school, and high school teachers who have greater numbers of students to teach, more specialized training, and more families to involve.

The school survey results have implications for building partnerships that deal with these topics. For example, more than 70% of the students say that they would like to be included in parent-teacher conferences, reflecting their needs to assume responsibility and maintain their autonomy. More than half of the students reported that they make decisions *alone* about their high school courses, perhaps reflecting autonomy, but also implying the need for more parent input in making such truly crucial decisions.

Among the high school teachers, 81% say that family involvement is important, and 33% say they personally strongly support it—but only 3% of them think that parents strongly support it. A major task of high school partnerships will be to convince these teachers that parents really do want to be involved and that the teachers can effectively involve most families. Survey data from parents such as that collected in these six high schools can help teachers see the similarities in family and school goals for better involvement.

Next Steps

The high schools in this project are already engaged in implementing new and improved practices for ninth-grade students and families and will follow up this work by extending the practices to inform and involve families throughout the grades. Examples of some of the practices they will be building are these:

- A five-session workshop series in which parents discuss teen behavior and appropriate parenting practices
- "Survival packets" given to each ninth-grade parent which include school telephone numbers, important meeting dates, school policies
- Students work on a "ten-year plan" for their futures and discuss their goals with a family member

Connors and Epstein suggest some "get started" steps for other urban, suburban, or rural high schools. Creating an "Action Team for School-Family-Community Partnerships" is the first step. Basic funding must then be secured (the project schools each have a small stipend per semester to work with).

The Action Team needs to get information about what partnership practices the school's teachers, students, and families are interested in pursuing. While gathering this information the team can begin selecting appropriate practices, including some basic ideas outlined by the high schools in this project. The researchers provide a chart of basic practices for the six types of school, family, and community partnerships that might be considered by "any high school" (see the next page "Any High School Can . . .").

Notes

1. From *Research and Development Report* (No. 5, pp. 1-4), edited by John H. Hollifield, June 1994. Baltimore: Center on Families, Communities, Schools and Children's Learning, Johns Hopkins University.

2. From *Trust Fund: School, Family, and Community Partnerships in High Schools* (Report No. 24) by Joyce L. Epstein and Lori J. Connors, 1994. Baltimore: Center on Families, Communities, Schools and Children's Learning, Johns Hopkins University.

3. From *Taking Stock: Views of Teachers, Parents, and Students on School, Family, and Community Partnerships in High Schools* (Report No. 25) by Lori J. Connors and Joyce L. Epstein, August 1994. Baltimore: Center on Families, Communities, Schools and Children's Learning, Johns Hopkins University.

Any High School Can . . .

Type 1 Parenting	Develop a lasting set of workshops on key issues in adolescent development. This could be a videotaped series, developed with the help of a local cable company, community or technical college, or the high school's media department. The guidance office could take leadership for these activities, working with the Action Team, perhaps using the tapes as a forum for a parent workshop series. The tapes can be made available to families through the school, the library, or for free at local video stores on a check-out basis.
Type 2 Communicating	Include students in parent-teacher conferences. Develop one-page guidelines for parents and teens to prepare for the conference. The guidelines would help parents and teens identify common concerns, interests, and talents to discuss with teachers during the conference. The conference could also focus on students' goals and how the teacher and parent could better assist the student.
Type 3 Volunteering	One member of the Action Team or a parent and teacher as co-chairs could coordinate parent and community volunteers with school and teacher needs for help. Encourage many to participate by allowing work to be done at home or at school, on weekends, or before/after regular school hours. Encourage teachers to be creative in their requests for assistance so that the many skills and interests of parents and community members can be tapped.
Type 4 Learning at Home	Design interactive homework that requires students to talk to someone at home about something interesting that they are learning in class or about important school decisions. The homework activity is the student's responsibility, but a parent or other family or community member is used as a reference source or audience for the student. This enables students to share ideas at the same time that families are informed about the students' curricula and learning activities.
Type 5 Decision Making	Invite parents and students to become members of school committees or councils to review curriculum or specific school policies. In order to encourage diverse representation, ask a more experienced parent or student leader to be a "buddy" to a less experienced parent or student.
Type 6 Collaborating With the Community	Develop a community resource directory, perhaps in cooperation with the school nurse, or with a member of the Chamber of Commerce or other group, which gives parents and students information on community agencies that can help with health issues, job training and summer or part-time employment for teens, and other areas of need for families and students.

Teachers Involve Parents in Schoolwork (TIPS) Processes

This section includes a summary of the *Teachers Involve Parents in Schoolwork (TIPS)* interactive homework process to assist elementary and middle schools with Type 4—Learning at Home. There also is a summary of TIPS Social Studies and Art, a process to help organize Type 3—Volunteering in the middle grades. The TIPS processes may be adapted to other grade levels and other subjects.

Teachers Involve Parents in Schoolwork (TIPS) Interactive Homework for the Elementary and Middle Grades

The Teachers Involve Parents in Schoolwork (TIPS) interactive homework process for the elementary and middle grades includes teachers' manuals and prototype homework assignments in math, science/health, and language arts.

Sample interactive homework assignments for high school students in math, English, history, geography, family life, health, and other subjects also are available from the Center. The samples were developed by one high school as part of its comprehensive program of partnerships.

Teachers Involve Parents in Schoolwork (TIPS) Social Studies and Art Volunteers for the Middle Grades

The TIPS Social Studies and Art process helps schools organize volunteers to integrate social studies and art in the middle grades. There is a manual for teacher and parent coordinators and sample presentations about artists and their work.

Involving Parents in Schoolwork
(TIPS) Processes

Joyce L. Epstein

Why Build School and Family Partnerships?

If enough studies show the same result, you begin to believe it. That is how it is with school and family partnerships. Research shows that parent involvement improves student achievement, attitudes, homework, report card grades, and aspirations. Surveys of parents show that most families want to be able to talk with, monitor, encourage, and guide their children as students, but they say they need more information from the schools about how to help their children at home.

Studies also show that when teachers guide involvement and interaction, more parents become involved in ways that benefit their children. For example, when teachers frequently use practices to involve families in reading, students gain more in reading than do similar students whose teachers do not involve families. This suggests an important connection between parent involvement in particular subjects and student success in those subjects. It also shows the important roles that teachers play in helping families become involved in schoolwork at home.

There are other benefits to school and family partnerships. When parents are assisted by the schools, they become more aware of their children's education and interact with their children more. Children see that their parents and teachers communicate. They become more aware that they can talk to someone at home about schoolwork and school decisions.

Based on research that links teachers' practices of involving families with more success for students, we developed a way for teachers to do this easily: Teachers Involve Parents in Schoolwork (TIPS). There are two TIPS processes—one that increases parent involvement *at home* on interactive homework assignments and one that increases parent involvement *at school* as volunteers.

Family Involvement at Home:
TIPS Interactive Homework in Math,
Science/Health, and Language Arts

Of all the types of involvement, the one that more parents want to know about is **How do I help my own child at home?** This request is at the top of parents' wish lists, as they want to do their part to help their children succeed in school each year. This most wanted involvement is one that schools often have had difficulty organizing. It requires every teacher at every grade level to communicate with families about how to work and interact with their children on learning at home.

To meet this need, teachers helped design, implement, and test TIPS interactive homework. With TIPS, any teacher can help all families stay informed and involved in their children's learning activities at home. With TIPS, students complete homework that should promote their success in school.

TIPS activities are **homework** assignments that **require** students to **talk to someone** at home about **something interesting** that they are **learning in class**. TIPS helps solve some important problems with homework. It enables all families to become involved, not just those who already know how to discuss math, science, or other subjects. The homework is the students' responsibility; parents are not asked to "teach" subjects or skills. TIPS requires students to share their work, ideas, and progress with their families. It asks families to comment on their children's work and to request other information from teachers in a section for home-to-school communication. With TIPS, homework becomes a three-way partnership involving students, families, and teachers.

One immediate result of this is that families recognize and appreciate the efforts of teachers to keep them informed and involved. The TIPS activities keep school on the agenda at home so that children know that their families believe schoolwork is important and worth talking about.

Overcoming Obstacles

JUMP HURDLE 1: HOMEWORK SHOULD
NOT ALWAYS BE DONE ALONE

Some teachers believe that all homework should be completed in a quiet place, away from the family or other people. Its purpose is to allow students to practice what was taught in class, to study for a quiz, or to complete other work *on their own*. While SOME homework is for these purposes, OTHER homework should fulfill other goals. TIPS homework—once a week in math or language arts, twice a month in science—is designed specifically to keep students and their families talking about schoolwork at home. More than quarterly report cards or lists of required skills or other occasional explanations, TIPS brings school home on a regular schedule of homework that requires children to talk with their parents and other family members.

JUMP HURDLE 2: JUST ANY HOMEWORK WON'T DO

Some homework is pretty boring; it requires students' time but not much thinking. TIPS activities must be challenging and engaging—the type of homework that students will want to explain and share with their families. TIPS includes higher-level thinking skills and interactions with family members that make students think, write, gather information, collect suggestions, explain, demonstrate, draw, sketch or construct things, and conduct other interactive activities with parents and other family members at home.

What Are TIPS Activities?

TIPS prototype activities are examples that teachers can use to design homework that matches the learning objectives for their students. There are TIPS prototype activities in math, science/health, and language arts.

TIPS Math provides a format for students to share what they are learning about a specific math skill. The TIPS format allows students to show parents exactly how they learned a skill in class. Then, they complete regular math homework activities and obtain parents' reactions. TIPS Math emphasizes the mastery of math skills—basic and advanced. The activities may include challenges in games or other extensions of skills or finding examples of the specific math skill in real life. TIPS Math homework should be assigned once a week to keep students and families talking about math at home on a regular schedule.

TIPS Science/Health provides a format for students to conduct and discuss a hands-on "lab" or data collection activity related to the science topics they study in class. In health, TIPS requires students to discuss topics, gather reactions, or collect data from family members on issues of health and student development. The hands-on science activities and interactive health assignments help students and their families see that these subjects are enjoyable, enriching, and part of everyday life.

In science, it is important that TIPS activities require only inexpensive or no-cost materials that are readily available at home. Special equipment, if it is ever needed, should be provided by the school. TIPS Science/Health activities include a brief letter to parents explaining the topic. Then, the activities outline objectives, materials, space for lab reports or data charts, challenges, discussion questions, conclusions, and home-to-school communication. TIPS Science/Health homework should be assigned on a regular schedule (e.g., once a week or twice a month) to keep students and families discovering and talking about science and health at home.

TIPS Language Arts provides a format for students to share a variety of skills in writing, reading, thinking, grammar, and related language activities. The students do the work—reading and writing—but students and parents enjoy thinking together, discussing, sharing, and exchanging ideas. Family members may listen to what their children write, help them edit their writing, think about words, react to writing, provide ideas, memories, and their own experiences, and other interactions. TIPS Language Arts homework should be assigned once a week to keep families aware of and involved in students' work and progress in language arts.

Some of the TIPS examples may be useful just as they are. But, because homework must match the teachers' learning objectives, most teachers will use the examples to help them design their own TIPS activities. After several years of development, TIPS now can be easily adopted or adapted. Teachers who see the activities usually say "I can do that!" That is exactly the reaction that will help every teacher in every grade level and every subject design interactive homework for their students and families.

How Do You Develop TIPS Homework?

TIPS can be developed in three clear steps:

- Teachers work together during the summer months to design and develop TIPS interactive homework assignments to match their own curricula and learning objectives.

- Teachers use the assignments with students and families throughout the school year.

- Revisions are made based on feedback from students, parents, and teachers using TIPS.

One way to develop TIPS is for a school or district to provide salary for a few teachers at each grade level to work together during the summer months. Support is needed for each teacher for two to four weeks to develop, edit, and produce the TIPS homework that will be used throughout the school year.

TIPS homework must be enjoyable as well as challenging. This takes some careful thinking about the design of homework and about how to build in students' communication with parents or other family members. It helps for two or more teachers to work together discussing, writing, and editing their ideas. It also helps if this work is guided by a curriculum supervisor, department chair, assistant principal, master or lead teacher, school-family coordinator, or other individual who can take the leadership role in developing and implementing TIPS.

Once tested, TIPS homework designs may be shared with other teachers or in other schools that follow the same curriculum objectives. Support for a few teachers in the summer, then, yields materials that can be used or adapted by many teachers for many years. The process is very cost-effective.

How Do You Implement TIPS Homework?

Teachers, students, parents, and administrators all have responsibilities for the success of TIPS:

- *Teachers* design the homework assignments or select those that match their classwork, orient parents to the process, explain TIPS and family involvement to students, follow-up homework in class, and maintain homework records.

- *Students* complete the TIPS assignments and involve their parents or other family members as directed in the activities.

- *Parents* learn about the TIPS process, set aside time each week to discuss TIPS homework activities with their children, and complete the home-to-school communication.

- *Principals* help teachers orient parents to the program and support and recognize teachers, students, and families who use TIPS well.

To introduce parents to TIPS, letters may be sent, newsletters can announce the interactive homework activities, and the process may be explained at parent-teacher meetings and conferences and at other occasions. Classroom or grade-level meetings may be conducted to show parents examples of the TIPS activities on an overhead projector and describe how they should proceed when their children bring TIPS activities home.

Students also must be oriented to the program and reminded about family involvement each time TIPS assignments are made. Teachers must reinforce that they want the children to talk with someone at home about the work and that they believe it is important for families to be aware of what children are learning in school.

How Do You Evaluate TIPS Homework?

There are two main goals for TIPS:

- To encourage students to complete their homework well and to improve attitudes, behaviors, and achievements

- To create good information and interactions at home between students and their families about schoolwork

TIPS homework comes with two "built in" evaluations. First, students are expected to complete the TIPS activities just as they do any homework. Teachers grade, return, and discuss TIPS just as they do other homework. Second, every TIPS activity includes a section called "home-to-school communication" so that parents can provide observations and reactions to their children's work. This section lets parents tell teachers if their children understood the homework or need extra help from the teacher, whether the assignment was enjoyable to parents and students at home, and if the activity informed parents about schoolwork in a particular subject. Teachers monitor parents' reactions and respond to questions with phone calls, notes, or individual meetings.

When educators use TIPS, they must evaluate whether and how the process helps them reach their goals for school and family connections. Follow-up activities are needed to learn whether parents need more information, explanations, or guidance in the use of TIPS at home and in their interactions with their children about schoolwork. This may be done with informal interviews, phone calls, or classroom or grade-level meetings with parents. Some informal and formal evaluations of TIPS have been conducted and reports are available.

How Do Parents, Students, and Teachers React to TIPS Homework?

TIPS is a special type of homework. The activities should be printed on colored paper to stand out from other paper in students' notebooks. One district using TIPS reported a parent's reaction: "When I see that yellow paper, I know that is important homework for my son to complete with me."

In Baltimore, interviews and surveys of parents, students, and teachers in the middle grades reveal overwhelmingly positive reactions. Parents say they get to talk about things with their children that they would otherwise not discuss. For example, when students worked on TIPS Language Arts, parents wrote,

> I can tell from Jenneaka relating the story to me that she really enjoyed reading it.

> Anthony is improving every day. I believe his report card will be better.

> This blue paper is a learning experience for me.

> Very interesting assignment. I enjoyed this and it brought back good memories.

When students worked on TIPS Science/Health, parents wrote,

> We are still working on neatness.

> Althea's thought process was more mature than what I knew.

> I think she could have done a better job with the consequences.

> This opened up an easier way of communicating.

Students say that they like TIPS because they do not have to copy the homework from the board, because it is not boring, and because they learn something from or about their parents or families that they did not know before. Most teachers report that more children complete TIPS than other homework.

Family Involvement at School as Volunteers: TIPS Social Studies and Art

A second TIPS process—**TIPS Social Studies and Art**—addresses the problem of organizing volunteers, especially in the middle grades. This process establishes a teacher-volunteer partnership to enrich the social studies curriculum for all students.

The TIPS Social Studies and Art process integrates art with social studies in the middle grades. The process brings volunteers (parents, other family members, or members of the community) to the school on a regular schedule to introduce artists and artwork to students. When students study American history in social studies, they see and learn about American artists; world history is linked to the work of artists from around the world; government and citizen participation is linked to artwork on themes of government and citizenship.

How Does TIPS Social Studies and Art Work?

Volunteers introduce a new print to students each month from October to May. Over three middle grades (e.g., 6-8 or 7-9) students are introduced to the work of at least 24 artists with different styles, media, and topics who lived at different times and places in history.

Presentations by parents or other volunteers on each art print require only 20 minutes of class time. Each presentation includes information on the artist's life, style and technique, the specific artwork, connections to social studies, and topics for class discussion, writing, and artwork. Research for the presentations may be conducted by parents who cannot volunteer at school but who want to contribute time and ideas to improve school programs. Discussions include anecdotes and interesting information about the artist and artwork that should interest middle grades students.

Why Implement TIPS Social Studies and Art?

TIPS Social Studies and Art is designed to increase students' knowledge, understanding, and appreciation of art, and to demonstrate connections of art with history, geography, and issues of importance in society. The TIPS process helps solve three common problems in the middle grades: the need for integrated or interdisciplinary curricula, the need for more productive parent volunteers, and the need for students to learn something about art as an important part of cultural literacy. The process is adaptable to other grade levels, other social studies units, and other subjects (e.g., art may be linked to English or literature or to foreign language classes or other subjects).

Prototype presentations in American History (14 artists), World Cultures (14 artists), and Government and Citizen Participation (12 artists) are available, along with a manual that outlines the work of teachers and parents to organize, implement, and evaluate the program. The presentations were designed by parents and other volunteers in partnership with teachers and researchers, tested by middle grades teachers, and evaluated in research. Prototype worksheets for students to use with field trips to art museums, sample quizzes to assess students' knowledge and reactions to the program, and questionnaires for teachers and volunteers about the program are included in the manual.

How Do You Implement TIPS Social Studies and Art?

The implementation process follows 10 easy steps:

1. **Select a teacher coordinator.** This is usually the Chair of the Social Studies Department, a team leader, or a social studies teacher who is committed to implementing an interdisciplinary program.

2. **Select a parent coordinator.** This is the person who coordinates the schedules of the parent volunteers and helps train the volunteers. There should also be an assistant parent coordinator who will assume the job the next school year.

3. **Order the prints** that fit the social studies curricula in Grades 6-8 or the middle grades in your school. Prints that are drymounted and laminated may be obtained for reasonable costs from Shorewood Fine Art Reproductions, Sandy Hook, Connecticut. There must be enough prints for the monthly rotations among teachers.

4. **Teachers select the art prints** to be presented and discussed by the volunteers.

5. **Recruit volunteers** to make classroom presentations once a month from October to May.

6. **Train the volunteers** so they are comfortable about their presentations. The manual helps with this training, making it possible to conduct the orientation session in about an hour.

7. **Schedule monthly presentations** at mutually convenient times for the volunteers and the teachers. Volunteers meet with the same classes each month.

8. **Coordinators check** with volunteers after the first visit and periodically throughout the year to see that the program is working as planned.

9. **Teachers evaluate students** to determine the benefits of the program for increasing knowledge of the artists and artwork and the development of understanding, appreciation, and criticism of art.

10. **Make necessary improvements** in the implementation process and continue the program.

These steps run smoothly as the parent coordinator and teacher coordinator become familiar with their roles and as a partnership develops between the volunteers and the teachers.

How Do You Get Started With TIPS Interactive Homework or Volunteers?

Teacher manuals and prototype activities are available to help any school understand and implement TIPS to increase parent involvement *at home* through interactive homework and *at school* through the organization of productive volunteers.

For **TIPS Interactive Homework,** there are manuals for teachers and prototype activities in math (Grades K-5) and science (Grade 3) in the elementary grades, and language arts, science/health, and math for the middle grades.

Teacher **Manual (elementary grades** for science and math) (J. Epstein and K. Salinas)	$ 8.00
TIPS **Math, Kindergarten**	$10.00
TIPS **Math, Grade 1**	$ 6.00
TIPS **Math, Grade 2**	$ 6.00
TIPS **Math, Grade 3**	$10.00
TIPS **Math, Grade 4**	$ 6.00
TIPS **Math, Grade 5**	$ 6.00
TIPS **Science, Grade 3**	$ 3.00
Teacher **Manual (middle grades** for language arts, science/health, and math) (J. Epstein, K. Salinas, V. Jackson, and Calverton and West Baltimore Middle Schools teachers)	$ 8.00
TIPS **Language Arts (Grade 6)** prototype packet	$ 8.00
TIPS **Science/Health (Grade 6)** prototype packet	$ 8.00
TIPS **Language Arts (Grade 7)** prototype packet	$ 8.00
TIPS **Science/Health (Grade 7)** prototype packet	$ 8.00
TIPS **Language Arts (Grade 8)** prototype packet	$ 8.00
TIPS **Science (Grade 8)** prototype packet	$ 8.00
TIPS **Math (Basic Skills)** prototype packet	$ 4.00

For **TIPS Social Studies and Art**, there are manuals and training materials for teacher and parent coordinators, and 40 prototype presentations on art prints for use with units in American History, World Cultures, and Government and Citizen Participation in the middle grades.

Teacher **Manual** Social Studies and Art (middle grades) (J. Epstein and K. Salinas)	$ 6.00
TIPS Presentations of Art Prints for	
American History (14 prototype presentations)	$ 6.00
World Cultures (14 prototype presentations)	$ 6.00
Government and Citizen Participation (12 prototype presentations)	$ 6.00

Use of TIPS activities requires the corresponding manual for teachers. Costs include shipping. In addition to these materials, a list and order form is available including about 50 articles, research reports, summaries, and questionnaires on school, family, and community partnerships.

To order the TIPS materials or to obtain a free list of available reports and materials, contact Diane Diggs, Publications, Center on School, Family, and Community Partnerships, Johns Hopkins University, 3505 North Charles Street, Baltimore, MD 21218. (Telephone: 410-516-8808)

NOTE: Research and development of TIPS Interactive Homework at the middle level was supported by a grant from the U.S. Department of Education, OERI, and the Edna McConnell Clark Foundation. Previous grants suppported R&D on TIPS at the elementary level. Research and development of TIPS Social Studies and Art Volunteers was supported by grants from OERI and the National Endowment for the Arts.

In *The School-Community Cookbook: Recipes for Successful Projects in the Schools* (pp. 176-182), edited by Carl S. Hyman, 1992. Baltimore, MD: Fund for Educational Excellence.

Surveys and Summaries:
Questionnaires on School
and Family Partnerships

Questionnaires for teachers and parents in the elementary grades and for teachers, parents, and students in high schools are available for Action Teams or others who want to gather reactions and hopes for improving school-family-community partnerships. The questionnaires come with forms to summarize data to help schools plan their programs of partnership.

Surveys and Summaries Help Schools Identify and Analyze Current Practices of Partnership; Develop More Comprehensive Programs[1]

More and more schools and districts are recognizing the need to develop effective parent, community, and school partnerships. They also are recognizing the need to first collect survey information about what their current practices are and what their parents, teachers, and even students think of those practices, other potential practices, and the need for and goals of parent involvement in general. Then the survey data must be analyzed and summarized to provide a base on which to build more comprehensive and successful partnerships among parents, community, and schools.

Center researchers Joyce L. Epstein, Lori J. Connors, and Karen Clark Salinas at Johns Hopkins University, in collaboration with Maryland teachers and administrators, have produced survey questionnaires to provide information for planning partnership projects. Forms are available to survey teachers and parents in elementary and middle schools and to survey teachers, parents, and students in high schools.

Teacher questionnaires ask teachers to provide professional judgments about parent involvement practices, what they are currently doing, and what programs they would like to see developed. *Parent questionnaires* ask parents to describe how they feel about the school, how they are currently participating, how well the school keeps them informed, and what practices they would like to see initiated. *Student questionnaires* ask high schoolers how they interact with their families on school matters, how the school helps their families to be involved, and what types of family-school partnerships they would like to see.

How to Carry Out a Survey

In addition to the survey questionnaires, the Center researchers have developed a step-by-step description of how to carry out an effective survey of teachers, parents, and students. The process includes reviewing the content of the questionnaires, deciding between doing a survey or using alternative methods to collect information (through panels, focus groups, breakfast meetings, or interviews), adding site-specific questions, preparing a cover letter, distributing and collecting the surveys, processing the data, analyzing and interpreting the data, discussing the results with the respondents, and then beginning the process of building a comprehensive program of school and family partnerships based on the data.

SUMMARIZE YOUR SURVEY DATA

For each question asked of teachers, parents, and students in the surveys, the researchers provide a form for summarizing and interpreting the responses. For example, Question 4 in the parent surveys asks parents to indicate how well the school provides them with information and involves them in activities. For 15 items ranging from "help me understand teen development" to "provide information on community services that I may want to use" parents of high school students indicate whether they think the school "should start" the practice, "could do better," or "does this very well now."

Parents' responses on Question 4 (and responses to parallel questions on the teacher and student surveys) provide raw data about how the school presently keeps them informed and encourages involvement, and what they would like to see done better in the future. The items in Question 4 cover the six major types of involvement in Epstein's framework for comprehensive programs of partnership.

The researchers provide a format for analyzing and summarizing data gathered from this question. First, for each item, you fill in a table to document the percentage of parents who responded "should start," "could do better," or "does well." In the next step, you circle the practices that receive over 40% of the parents' responses. This provides a quick profile of what your school's parents perceive to be strong, weak, and needed practices.

This summarization and interpretation process is followed for each question asked of parents, teachers, and students. A format is then provided for integrating the information from each group of respondents into a list of practices that all agree need to be improved or need to be added to the school and family partnership plan at the school.

The surveys and reports on the reliability of scales based on items from the questionnaires are available from the Center.[2]

School and Family Partnerships: Surveys and Summaries
(revised 1993)

- Questionnaires for Teachers and Parents in Elementary and Middle Grades

- How to Summarize Your School's Survey Data

Joyce L. Epstein and Karen Clark Salinas. (P-8-3, $8.00)

High School and Family Partnerships: Surveys and Summaries (1993)

- Questionnaires for Teachers, Parents, and Students
- How to Summarize Your High School's Survey Data

Joyce L. Epstein, Lori J. Connors, and Karen Clark Salinas.
    (P-8-4, $8.00)

Reliabilities and Summaries of Scales From Surveys of Teachers and Parents in the Elementary and Middle Grades (1994)

Joyce L. Epstein, Karen Clark Salinas, and Carrie S. Horsey.
    (P-8-5, $2.00)

Reliabilities and Summaries of Scales From Surveys of Teachers, Parents, and Students in High School (Grade 9) (1995)

Joyce L. Epstein, Lori Connors-Tadros, Carrie S. Horsey,
    and Beth S. Simon. (P-8-6, $2.00)

Note

1. Reprinted from *Research and Development Report* No. 4 (1993). Surveys and summaries help schools identify and analyze current practices of partnership; develop more comprehensive programs. John H. Hollifield (ed.). Baltimore: Center on Families, Communities, Schools and Children's Learning, Johns Hopkins University.

2. To order the surveys and related documents, contact Diane Diggs, Publications, Center or School, Family and Community Partnerships, Johns Hopkins University, 3505 North Charles Street, Baltimore, MD 21218. (Telephone: 410-516-8808)

8

Networking for Best Results

National Network. You may use this handbook on your own to help you develop a comprehensive program of school-family-community partnerships. Or you may want to join the National Network of Partnership-2000 Schools at Johns Hopkins University. The **Partnership-2000 Schools Summary** describes the requirements and services of the National Network and how to join.

Update: Annual Progress Report. Each year, the Partnership-2000 Schools staff communicates with school, district, and state members of the National Network to document progress toward the goals they set for school-family-community partnerships.

Newsletters. Twice each year, members receive *Type 2,* the newsletter of the National Network of Partnership-2000 Schools. Each issue includes information about successful practices of school-family-community partnerships and focuses on topics raised in communications with members of the National Network.

Sharing Best Practices (optional). The Sharing Best Practices of School-Family-Community Partnerships Forms are guides for schools, districts, and states that would like to report effective practices of partnership.

Focus on Results (optional). Each year, members of the National Network are invited to join a cross-site exploration called Focus on Results. The purpose is to learn how practices of school-family-community partnerships help schools reach specific goals. Members may voluntarily join the cross-site project to learn *which practices* produce *measurable results* for students, families, and schools.

Workshops for Key Contacts (optional). Twice each year (March and June), the Partnership-2000 Schools staff conducts optional training workshops at Johns Hopkins University for the Key Contacts of the states, districts, and schools in the National Network.

National Network of Partnership-2000 Schools

Joyce L. Epstein
Director, Center on School, Family, and Community Partnerships
Johns Hopkins University

Educators and families agree that school-family-community partnerships are essential for children's success. Based on more than a decade of research and the work of many educators, parents, students, and others, we know that it is possible for all elementary, middle, and high schools to develop and maintain strong programs of partnership. As a member of the National Network of Partnership-2000 Schools, you will be encouraged, informed, recognized, and supported in your efforts to improve and maintain school, family, and community connections.

What is the National Network of Partnership-2000 Schools?

Established by researchers at Johns Hopkins University in 1996, the National Network of Partnership-2000 Schools brings together schools, districts, and states that are committed to developing and maintaining strong programs of school-family-community partnerships. Each Partnership-2000 School strengthens its program by addressing six types of involvement and by using an Action Team approach. Districts and states assist increasing numbers of schools to conduct these activities.

Why Become a Member of Partnership-2000 Schools?

Membership has its benefits! Members of the Network receive support for their partnership efforts. For each school, district, and state that joins the National Network, this Center will do the following:

- ★ Supply a manual to guide the work of Action Teams
- ★ Issue a Certificate of Membership
- ★ Conduct semi-annual training workshops at Johns Hopkins
- ★ Distribute *Type 2*, the Network's semi-annual newsletter
- ★ Provide technical assistance by phone, e-mail, and web site
- ★ Offer optional research and evaluation opportunities

Members benefit from the experience of others in the Network, too. In every edition of the newsletter, at training workshops, and through the Partnership-2000 Schools web site, members have opportunities to share best practices, challenges, and creative options for improving school-family-community connections.

Who May Join the National Network of Partnership-2000 Schools?

Membership is open to all states, districts, intermediate units, and schools that agree to the required components listed on the following page.

Membership Requirements

Developing good connections between home, school, and community is an on-going process that takes time, organization and effort. The National Network of Partnership-2000 Schools offers a research-based framework and strategies that enable all schools to organize productive school-family-community partnerships to help students succeed. Members may add other creative elements to expand their programs.

Members of the Network will work with this Center to improve connections with students, families, and communities. There is no membership fee to join the Network, but schools, districts, and states must meet a few requirements.

At the SCHOOL LEVEL, each Partnership-2000 School will:

✓ Create an Action Team for School, Family, and Community Partnerships.

✓ Use the framework of six types of involvement to plan and implement a program of partnerships.

✓ Allocate an annual budget for the work and activities of the school's Action Team.

At the DISTRICT LEVEL, each Partnership-2000 District will:

✓ Assign the equivalent of one full-time facilitator to work with 15 to 25 schools to create their Action Teams for Partnerships. Part-time coordinators may work in districts with fewer tnan 15 schools.

✓ Allocate an annual budget for the District's work and activities to develop, strengthen, and maintain programs of partnership in all schools.

✓ Assist each participating school to fulfill the requirements listed above for the school level.

At the STATE LEVEL, each Partnership-2000 State will:

✓ Identify or create an office, department, or division that will take leadership for helping all districts and schools to develop programs of partnership. This division must have at least one professional full-time-equivalent (FTE) leader and adequate professional and support staff to coordinate and conduct state-level activities for school, family, and community partnerships.

✓ Allocate an annual budget for the work of this office and the activities to support the districts and schools in the project.

✓ Assist the participating districts and/or schools to fulfill the requirements listed above for the district and school levels.

ALL MEMBERS will:

✓ Communicate with the Center annually to share progress and plans to continue in the Network.

If your school, district, or state is ready to take action to develop and maintain strong school, family, and community partnerships, you are invited to join the National Network of Partnership-2000 Schools. To receive more information and membership forms for schools, districts, or states, write to Dr. Joyce Epstein, Director, Center on School, Family, and Community Partnerships, 3505 North Charles Street, Baltimore, MD 21218. Or contact Karen Salinas at Tel: 410-516-8818 or Fax: 410-516-8890. Or e-mail, p2000@csos.jhu.edu.

Please visit us on the Internet at http://www.csos.jhu.edu/p2000

SHARING BEST PRACTICES OF
SCHOOL-FAMILY-COMMUNITY PARTNERSHIPS

_____ SCHOOL YEAR

(An Optional Activity for the National Network of Partnership-2000 Schools)

Please complete the following information and attach this page when you submit your outline and story.

Name of School: _____

School Address: _____

Reporter: _____

    Position on Action Team: _____

    Phone: _____

Title of Best Practice: _____

Please check your preference:

❑ YES, our best practice may be summarized and shared with others, including our school name and contact information.

❑ NO, please do not summarize or share our best practice with others until you contact us.

Signatures:

_____   _____

Principal   **Action Team Chair**

Send your **OUTLINE and STORY** to:

Karen Clark Salinas
Communications Director
National Network of Partnership-2000 Schools
Johns Hopkins University
3505 North Charles Street
Baltimore, MD 21218

Fax: 410-516-8890

Sharing Best Practices of
School-Family-Community Partnerships

Do you have a school-family-community partnership activity that is working very well? Use the following guide to submit information on each best practice of partnerships that you want to share with other members of the National Network of Partnership-2000 Schools.

Examples of best practices will be selected from submissions that are well written, meet the challenges set for each type of involvement, and include clear evidence of effects on students, families, teaching practice, or school climate. There are two parts to your report: **an outline that lists the facts** about an activity and **a narrative that tells the story** about your particularly successful practice.

LIST THE FACTS...

Organization and Implementation

- What is the specific goal(s) of this practice?

- How does this practice support your school improvement goals?

- Which of the six types of involvement does it include?

- Which grade level(s) are involved in this practice? How many students, families, teachers, or others are directly involved?

- How is the practice organized and conducted?

- What materials or resources are required? What are the real and hidden "costs" of the practice? From where do you obtain the needed funds or resources?

- What training, orientation, and follow-ups are required?

- When was this practice first implemented in your school?

Results

- What clear evidence do you have that the practice has reached (or is moving toward) its goal(s)?

- What results were observed or measured? How were these results measured?

- Do you have plans for a formal evaluation of this practice? If so, outline briefly.

Improvements

- What improvements have been made over time in the design and implementation of this practice <u>OR</u> what changes should be made to improve the practice in the future?

- What is most difficult about implementing this practice?

- What challenges or problems did your school face and how were they solved? Or, what challenges might other schools face in implementing this practice and how might they overcome the challenges?

- What are the next steps for improving this practice in your school?

Additional Information

- What anecdotes do you want to share about the design, implementation, or results of the practice?

- What other important information do you have about reactions of or support from teachers, parents, students, or community members?

TELL YOUR STORY....

From your outline, write a narrative of *2-4 double-spaced,* **typed** *pages* to explain your best practice so that others may adopt or adapt it for their partnership programs. (For examples, see Chapter 2.)

You may use your own format to present an easy-to-understand report based on your outline of important facts, or you may use the following guide.

Title: Give your narrative a catchy title for the practice you are sharing.

1. *Background and Purpose*—What is the practice? What was the reason for adding this practice to your school's program of partnerships? When did you begin this practice?

2. *Design and Implementation*—What did you actually do? Describe how the practice was implemented—e.g., by how many teachers, to reach which families and students? What challenges did you meet in implementing this activity, and how did you overcome the challenges? Or, what challenges might others meet? What improvements are anticipated as the practice continues? Include anecdotes on *implementation* in this section.

3. *Results*—What happened because of this practice? How was it received? How well was it implemented? What did parents, teachers, students, and others say or do differently because of this practice? What results were observed? Were any results formally measured? How did this practice assist your school with a specific school improvement goal? Include anecdotes on *results* in this section.

4. *Budget*—How much did it cost to design and implement this practice? Where did you get the funds and resources?

5. *Any other crucial information*—You may include one or two photos or one or two sample printed pages that can be easily reproduced.

District Leadership

SHARING BEST PRACTICES OF
SCHOOL-FAMILY-COMMUNITY PARTNERSHIPS

(An Optional Activity for the National Network of Partnership-2000 Schools)

Please complete the following information and attach this page when you submit your outline and story.

Name of District: _____

District Address: _____

Reporter: _____

    Position: _____

    Phone: _____

Title of Best Practice: _____

Please check your preference:

❏   YES, our best practice may be summarized and shared with others, including our district name and contact information.

❏   NO, please do not summarize or share our best practice with others until you contact us.

Signature:

_____   _____

Key Contact   **Date**

Send your **OUTLINE and STORY** to:

Karen Clark Salinas
Communications Director
National Network of Partnership-2000 Schools
Johns Hopkins University
3505 North Charles Street
Baltimore, MD 21218

Fax: 410-516-8890

Sharing Best Practices of
School-Family-Community Partnerships

Have you designed and implemented a successful **district leadership activity** that directly supports and assists your districts or schools with their work on school, family, and community partnerships?

You may have best practices in:

(a) policy—e.g., how your written policy was developed, or how various district departments cooperate on school, family, and community partnerships;

(b) funding—e.g., how your district funds your position, facilitators, and Action Teams;

(c) technical assistance—e.g., how facilitators meet with and guide Action Teams, how you organize district-wide newsletters or workshops for schools to share their best practices or plans for the next school year; or

(d) other district-level activities.

Examples of best practices will be selected from submissions that are well written and that clearly show how district leaders directly support individual schools or all schools and families in the district. Please use the following guide to submit information on each best practice of school, family, and community partnerships that you want to share with other DISTRICT leaders in the National Network of Partnership-2000 Schools. There are two parts to your report: an outline that lists the facts about your leadership activity and a narrative that tells the story about your particularly successful practice.

LIST THE FACTS...

Organization and Implementation

- What is the specific goal(s) of this practice?

- How does this practice support or facilitate the work of schools or families in your district?

- Which grade level(s) are targeted by this practice? How many schools, teachers, families, students, and others are directly involved?

- How is the practice organized and conducted?

- What materials or resources are required? What are the real and hidden "costs" of the practice? From where do you obtain the funds or resources?

- What training, orientation, and follow-ups are required?

- When was this practice first implemented by your district?

Results

- What clear evidence do you have that the practice has reached (or is moving toward) its goal(s)?

- What results were observed or measured? How were these results measured?

- Do you have plans for a formal evaluation of this practice? If so, explain.

Improvements

- What improvements have been made over time in the design and implementation of this practice *or* what changes should be made to improve the practice in the future?

- What is most difficult about implementing this practice?

- What challenges or problems did your district face and how were they solved? Or, what challenges might other districts face in implementing this practice and how might they overcome the challenges?

- What are the next steps for improving this practice in your district?

Additional Information

- What anecdotes do you want to share about the design, implementation, or results of the practice?

- What other important information do you have about reactions of or support from district or state staff, schools, families, or the community?

TELL YOUR STORY....

From your outline, write a narrative of *2-4 double-spaced,* **typed** *pages* to explain your best practice so that others may adopt or adapt it for their partnership programs. You may use your own format to present an easy-to-understand report based on your outline of important facts, or you may use the following guide.

Title: Give your narrative a catchy title for the practice you are sharing.

1. *Background and Purpose*—What is the practice? What was the reason for adding this practice to your district's program of partnerships? When did you begin this practice?

2. *Design and Implementation*—What did you actually do? Describe how the practice was implemented—e.g., to reach which schools, families, or students? What challenges did you meet in implementing this activity, and how did you overcome the challenges? Or, what challenges might others meet? What improvements are anticipated as the practice continues? Include anecdotes on *implementation* in this section.

3. *Results*—What happened because of this practice? How was it received? How well was it implemented? What did district staff, schools, families, and others say or do differently because of this practice? What results were observed? Were any results formally measured? How did this practice assist your district with a specific goal? Include anecdotes on *results* in this section.

4. *Budget*—How much did it cost to design and implement this practice? Where did you get the funds and resources?

5. *Any other crucial information*—You may include one or two photos or one or two sample printed pages that can be easily reproduced.

State Leadership

SHARING BEST PRACTICES OF
SCHOOL-FAMILY-COMMUNITY PARTNERSHIPS

(An Optional Activity for the National Network of Partnership-2000 Schools)

Please complete the following information and attach this page when you submit your outline and story.

Name of State Department of Education: _____

Mailing Address: _____

Reporter: _____

    Position: _____

    Phone: _____

Title of Best Practice: _____

Please check your preference:

❑ YES, our best practice may be summarized and shared with others, including our name and contact information.

❑ NO, please do not summarize or share our best practice with others until you contact us.

Signature:

_____   _____

Key Contact   **Date**

Send your **OUTLINE and STORY** to:

Karen Clark Salinas
Communications Director
National Network of Partnership-2000 Schools
Johns Hopkins University
3505 North Charles Street
Baltimore, MD 21218

Fax: 410-516-8890

Sharing Best Practices of
School-Family-Community Partnerships

Have you designed and implemented a successful state leadership activity that directly supports and assists your districts or schools with their work on school, family, and community partnerships?

You may have best practices in:

(a) policy development or how various divisions in the state department cooperate on school, family, and community partnerships;

(b) funding—e.g., how your state pays for your position and other staff, or awards grants to districts and/or schools;

(c) technical assistance—e.g., how facilitators meet with and guide district or school leaders about school, family, and community partnerships, how you organize state-level newsletters, training workshops, or conferences for districts or schools to share their best practices or plans for the next school year; or

(d) other state-level activities.

Examples of best practices will be selected from submissions that are well written and that clearly show how state leaders directly support districts and/or schools, or provide leadership and technical assistance to districts, schools, and families across the state. Please use the following guide to submit information on each best practice of school, family, and community partnerships that you want to share with other STATE leaders in the National Network of Partnership-2000 Schools. There are two parts to your report: an outline that lists the facts about your leadership activity and a narrative that tells the story about your particularly successful practice.

LIST THE FACTS...

Organization and Implementation

- What is the specific goal(s) of this practice?

- How does this practice support or facilitate the work of districts or schools in your state?

- Which grade level(s) are targeted by this practice? How many districts or schools are directly involved?

- How is the practice organized and conducted?

- What materials or resources are required? What are the real and hidden "costs" of the practice? From where do you obtain the funds or resources?

- What training, orientation, and follow-ups are required?

- When was this practice first implemented by your state?

Results

- What clear evidence do you have that the practice has reached (or is moving toward) its goal(s)?

- What results were observed or measured? How were these results measured?

- Do you have plans for a formal evaluation of this practice? If so, explain.

Improvements

- What improvements have been made over time in the design and implementation of this practice *or* what changes should be made to improve the practice in the future?

- What is most difficult about implementing this practice?

- What challenges or problems did your state face and how were they solved? Or, what challenges might other states face in implementing this practice and how might they overcome the challenges?

- What are the next steps for improving this practice in your state?

Additional Information

- What anecdotes do you want to share about the design, implementation, or results of the practice?

- What other important information do you have about reactions of or support from other state staff, districts, or schools?

TELL YOUR STORY....

From your outline, write a narrative of *2-4 double-spaced,* **typed** pages to explain your best practice so that others may adopt or adapt it for their partnership programs. You may use your own format to present an easy-to-understand report based on your outline of important facts, or you may use the following guide.

Title: Give your narrative a catchy title for the practice you are sharing.

1. *Background and Purpose*—What is the practice? What was the reason for adding this practice to your state's program of partnerships? When did you begin this practice?

2. *Design and Implementation*—What did you actually do? Describe how the practice was implemented—e.g., to reach which districts or schools? What challenges did you meet in implementing this activity, and how did you overcome the challenges? Or, what challenges might others meet? What improvements are anticipated as the practice continues? Include anecdotes on *implementation* in this section.

3. *Results*—What happened because of this practice? How was it received? How well was it implemented? What did districts or schools say or do differently because of this practice? What results were observed? Were any results formally measured? How did this practice assist your state with a specific goal? Include anecdotes on *results* in this section.

4. *Budget*—How much did it cost to design and implement this practice? Where did you get the funds and resources?

5. *Any other crucial information*—You may include one or two photos or one or two sample printed pages that can be easily reproduced.

Workshops for Key Contacts

Optional training workshops for Key Contacts from states, districts, and schools in the National Network of Partnership-2000 Schools are conducted each year at Johns Hopkins University in March and June. There is no charge for these workshops, but participants must arrange and pay for their own travel, hotel, meals, and other expenses. This handbook contains all of the information needed to develop comprehensive programs of partnership that include all six types of involvement using an Action Team approach. The optional training workshops provide extra initial guidance and opportunities to discuss ideas with other Key Contacts in the National Network and the Partnership-2000 Schools staff. The two-day workshops assist participants to conduct training workshops with their schools and to move forward with their program development activities at the school, district, and state levels.

The workshops address such questions as these:

- What are the six types of involvement and what challenges must be met to successfully implement each type of involvement?

- Who serves on Action Teams for School, Family, and Community Partnerships, and what are their responsibilities?

- How do three-year outlines and one-year action plans help schools make real progress in school-family-community partnerships?

- What is the work of the "Key Contact" at the state, district, and school levels?

- How do school-family-community partnership activities support school improvement plans and help reach school goals?

- What state, district, and school budgets are available to support the development of programs of partnership?

- How do schools, districts, and states share ideas, document results, and monitor progress?

Additional topics are collected from the participants to ensure that the workshops address their specific questions. There are opportunities for those attending to share information about their present programs and successful practices of partnership.

One-on-one time is scheduled with Partnership-2000 Schools staff as needed to discuss the unique challenges of members' sites.

Members of the National Network of Partnership-2000 Schools are notified about all training workshops held at Johns Hopkins University.

For information about future workshops, contact Karen Clark Salinas, Communications Director, 410-516-8818.

Suggested Readings

For more information, see the research and practical references in Chapters 1 and 7. Also, the following recent publications from the Center may be helpful:

Ames, C., De Stefano, L., Watkins, T., & Sheldon, S. (1995). *Teachers' school-to-home communications and parent involvement: The role of parent perceptions and beliefs* (Report No. 28). Baltimore: Center on Families, Communities, Schools and Children's Learning, Johns Hopkins University.

Brady, P., & Mighty, R., with Davies, D. (1996). *A tale of two partnerships* [Video]. Baltimore: Center on Families, Communities, Schools and Children's Learning, Johns Hopkins University.

Burch, P., Palanki, A., with Davies, D. (1995). *From clients to partners: Four case studies of collaboration and family involvement in the development of school-linked services* (Report No. 29). Baltimore: Center on Families, Communities, Schools and Children's Learning, Johns Hopkins University.

Connors-Tadros, L. (1996). *Effects of Even Start on family literacy: Local and national comparisons* (Report No. 35). Baltimore: Center on Families, Communities, Schools and Children's Learning, Johns Hopkins University.

Delgado-Gaitan, C. (1994). *Empowerment in Carpinteria: A five-year study of family, school, and community partnerships* (Report No. 49). Baltimore: Center for Research on Effective Schooling for Disadvantaged Students.

Epstein, J. L., Herrick, S. C., & Coates, L. (1996). Effects of summer home learning packets on student achievement in language arts in the middle grades. *School Effectiveness and School Improvement, 7*(3), 93-120.

Epstein, J. L., & Hollifield, J. L. (1996). Title I and school-family-community partnerships: Using research to realize the potential. *Journal of Education for Students Placed at Risk (JESPAR), 1*(3), 263-279.

Hidalgo, N., Bright, J., Siu, S. F., Swap, S. M., & Epstein, J. L. (1995). Research on families, schools, and communities: A multicultural perspective. In J. Banks (Ed.), *Handbook of research on multicultural education* (pp. 498-524). New York: Macmillan.

Johnson, V. R. (1992). *Building community: How to start a family center in your school* [Video]. Baltimore: Center on Families, Communities, Schools and Children's Learning, Johns Hopkins University.

Johnson, V. R. (1996). *Family center guidebook.* Baltimore: Center on Families, Communities, Schools and Children's Learning, Johns Hopkins University.

Nettles, S. M. (1994). *Coaching in communities: A practitioner's manual.* Baltimore: Center on Families, Communities, Schools and Children's Learning, Johns Hopkins University.

Sanders, M. G. (1996). Action teams in action: Interviews and observations in three schools in the Baltimore School-Family-Community Partnership Program. *Journal of Education for Students Placed at Risk (JESPAR), 1*(3), 49-262.

Sanders, M. G. (1996). Building family partnerships that last. *Educational Leadership, 54*(3), 61-65.

Siu, S. F. (1996). *Questions and answers: What research says about the education of Chinese-American children.* Baltimore: Center on Families, Communities, Schools and Children's Learning, Johns Hopkins University.

These reports, reprints, and videos are available from the Center. For publications lists and information on ordering, contact Diane Diggs, Publications, Center on School, Family, and Community Partnerships/CRESPAR, Johns Hopkins University, 3505 North Charles Street, Baltimore, MD 21218. Phone: 410-516-8808; Fax: 410-516-8890.

These recent research and practical publications also may be of interest:

Carey, N., & Farris, E. (1996). *Parents and schools: Partners in student learning* (Statistics in Brief, OERI-NCES No. 96-913). Washington, DC: U.S. Department of Education.

Goodman, J. F., Sutton, V., & Harkavy, I. (1995). The effectiveness of family workshops in a middle school setting. *Phi Delta Kappan, 76*(9), 694-700.

Hoover-Dempsey, K. V., & Sandler, H. M. (1995). Parental involvement in children's education: Why does it make a difference? *Teachers College Record, 97*(2), 310-331.

Landsverk, R. (1996). *Families • Communities • Schools learning together* (Series of bulletins). Madison: Wisconsin Department of Public Instruction.

National Educational Goals Panel. (1995). *Executive summary: Improving education through family-school-community partnerships.* Washington, DC: Author.

National Parent-Teacher Association. (1997). *National parent and family involvement program standards.* Chicago: Author.

Turnbull, A. P., & Turnbull, H. R. (1996). *Families, professionals, and exceptionality: A special partnership.* Upper Saddle River, NJ: Merrill.

Vaden-Kiernan, N. (1996). *Parents' reports of school practices to involve families* (Statistics in Brief, OERI-NCES No. 97-327). Washington, DC: U.S. Department of Education.

U.S. Department of Education. (1994). *Strong families, strong schools: Building community partnerships for learning.* Washington, DC: Author.

To order more copies of this book fill out the form below!

ORDER FORM

D7818

(For faster service, photocopy this form and send with your P.O.)

CORWIN PRESS, INC.
A Sage Publications Company
2455 Teller Road
Thousand Oaks, CA 91320-2218
Federal ID Number 77-0260369

(Professional books may be tax-deductible.)

Call: 805-499-9774 or
Fax: 805-499-0871 or
E-mail: order@corwin.sagepub.com
http://www.sagepub.com/sagepage/
corwin.htm

Ship to

Name _____

Title _____

Institution _____

Address _____

City _____ State _____ ZIP + 4 _____

Telephone (*Required* for bill-me orders) (_____) _____

Bill to (if different) _____ **P.O.** _____

Institution _____

Attn. _____

Address _____

City _____ State _____ ZIP + 4 _____

Method of Payment

❑ Check enclosed # _____   ❑ **VISA**   ❑ **MasterCard**

_____
Account Number   Exp. Date

_____
Signature

❑ My order exceeds $25.00, please bill me.

❑ Please send me information on _____

Qty.	Title	Book No.	Unit Price	Amount
	School, Family, and Community Partnerships: **Your Handbook for Action**	**6571-0 (Paper)**	**$29.95**	
		6570-2 (Cloth)	**$69.95**	

Total Book Order	
In CA, add 7¼% Sales Tax	
In IL, add 6¼% Sales Tax	
In MA, add 5% Sales Tax	
In NY, add appropriate Sales Tax	
In Canada, add 7% GST*	
Subtotal	
Handling Charges*	
Amount Due	

* Shipping and handling charges are $3.50 for the first book and $1.00 for each additional book. These charges apply to all orders, including purchase orders and those prepaid by check or credit card. All orders are shipped Ground Parcel unless otherwise requested. Discounts are available for quantity orders — call Customer Service. Prices subject to change without notice. **In Canada, please add 7% GST (12978 6448 RT) and remit in U.S. dollars.** Thank you.

CORWIN
PRESS

The Corwin Press logo—a raven striding across an open book—represents the happy union of courage and learning. We are a professional-level publisher of books and journals for K–12 educators, and we are committed to creating and providing resources that embody these qualities. Corwin's motto is "Success for All Learners."